Pangyrus

Pangyrus © 2018
All Stories © 2017
Attributed to the authors named herein, except when noted otherwise
under "Acknowledgements"
ISBN: 978-0-9979164-3-0

For information about permission to reproduce selections from this book,
please write to Permissions at info@pangyrus.com

The text of this book is set in Palatino
with display text set in Crimson and Baskerville
Composition by Yahya Chaudhry and Abraar Chaudhry
Cover design by Orpha Rivera

Editor: Greg Harris
Managing Editor: Cynthia Bargar
Fiction Editors: Anne Bernays, Sarah Colwill-Brown, Erica Boyce Murphy
Poetry Editor: Cheryl Clark Vermeulen
Nonfiction Editors: E.B. Bartels, Jess McCann
Food Editor: Deborah Norkin
Science Editor: Mona Tousian
Comics Editor: Dan Mazur
Contributing Editors: Kalpana Jain, Carmen Nobel
Reviews Editor: Chris Hartman
Social Media Director: Yahya Chaudhry
Graphic & Web Designer: Esther Weeks
Readers and Copy Editors: Chris Hartman, Ahna Wayne Aposhian,
Graeme Harcourt, Robert Olechna, Molly Howes
Business Manager: Lakeisha Landrum
Editorial Assistants: Sam Piscitelli, Suzannah Lutz
Logo Design: Ted Ollier

Pangyrus
79 JFK Street, L103
Cambridge, MA 02138
pangyrus.com

Contents

Pangyrus

Note from the Editor

"No words." So often that's our response on social media to the latest outrage. And the outrages come thick and heavy. Lies. Emoluments. Corruption. Assault. In the name of division and hatred, vote suppression and news suppression and protest suppression. Misogyny. The turn against immigrants, when we were all immigrants except Native Americans. The contempt for Native Americans.

Actual goddamn Nazis in the streets of a university town.

Well, we have the words. And the comics. Against the cynical manipulation of the headlines, against what Iris Murdoch warns us is the enemy of moral life, "the fat, relentless ego," we ask here, what does it look and sound like to remember our shared humanity, to stand up for truths, to undercut political marketing with what Murdoch reminds us is its opposite: "a refined and honest perception of what is really the case, a patient and just discernment and exploration of what confronts one, which is the result not simply of opening one's eyes but of a certain and perfectly familiar kind of moral discipline."

The vision that led to this issue of *Pangyrus* predates Trump's presidency. Launched (and still edited) from my office in Harvard's Kennedy School of Government, *Pangyrus* took shape and adopted its tagline, "Stories Connect Here," amidst the rich dialogues and the transformative experiences of those who, by and large, hope to make government by the people work for the people. Anguished discussion arose during the Syrian refugee crisis in 2015: what to do? In collaboration with the brilliant and wonderful

Uzra Khan, editor of the Kennedy School Review, we put together a spoken-word event on the theme of "displacement." Speakers who had grown up as refugees, as oppressed minorities, who had invested whole careers in humanitarian efforts, arose to give a human face to the shocking numbers of displaced peoples. The event was personal, and inspirational, one of the most moving I've ever attended. Richard Parker, historian and co-founder of *Mother Jones* and, I'm proud to say, a fellow faculty member and friend, gave the event its grace note, reminding of the origin of the quote Martin Luther King, Jr. and then Obama made famous, that "the moral arc of the universe is long, but it bends towards justice." It came from the abolitionist movement, and from Theodore Parker, his ancestor, who--though a white Anglo-Saxon religious figure, Richard noted with humor--had struggled to birth in America a notion of justice that rejected racial division.

The moderators of that event, and the public speaking lecturers who'd helped many of the students achieve their power at the podium, were *Pangyrus* nonfiction editor Marie Danziger and our all-time most-read author Tim McCarthy. It was Tim and fellow writer Sarah Sweeney who, two years later, called to confront a crisis as grave as any America has faced in our lifetime, revived the spoken-word format, and convinced the American Repertory Theater at Harvard to host a series at OBERON theater under the auspices of the A.R.T. of Human Rights series. On November 16, 2017, we launched "Resistance Mic!"

If you have not yet been to Resistance Mic!, I need to paint the picture. OBERON, in Harvard Square, is an experimental space, a theater-in-a-night-club, where every Saturday night *A Midsummer Night's Dream* struts to life the way Shakespeare never intended it, as a disco experience with aerial silk and roller blades.

So too Resistance Mic! is experimental, improvisational. We've had poets inspired by the space and the scene compose spoken-word pieces in the green room just before hitting the stage. We opened the first season with a dramatic reading of the Declaration of Independence ("When in the Course of human events, it becomes necessary for one people to dissolve the political bands which have connected them with another...") and closed on Robert Pinsky and Stan Strickland's swirling, incantatory, saxophone-infused "Battle Hymn of the Republic" trampling out the vintage where the grapes of wrath are stored.

In between we had comic monologues about an African child in America (mis)learning about her home country through Disney's *The Lion King*, and about dating across the political divide. Musicians who entranced, from the Kuumba Singers' 30+ voices shaking OBERON to its foundations, to Davóne Tines imploring "Saint Martin, Saint Thurgood, Saint Malcolm" to SPEAK, in a voice that also shook OBERON to its foundations (How is this place still standing?).

Above all we had *writers* doing what writers do: giving the words to things we feel, noticing the things we miss. Stephanie Burt finding civilization in a mall's dash of natural life. Krysten Hill's razor-edged "sorries." Steve Almond undercutting the hate speech with humor and humanity. Sonya Larson facing us with questions of race deeper than skin color. Anne Champion standing her ground for a decency we feared already lost, for a politics in which angry insult can be turned, with even more anger, back to honor.

I'm proud to say you can now read in this volume many of the great pieces we heard. Boyah Farah's memoir of life in refugee camps, and his gentle warning to an America that finds such experiences remote. Kazim Ali's plea to "Somehow still their war hungry violins." Seno Gumira Ajidarma's surreal "Eyewitness," on perversion of justice. Jenna Blum's drawing historical parallels to another authoritarian liar. Sari Boren's graceful, deep look at how we wrestle with the legacy of slavery in our National Parks. Sebastian Johnson's anguished "The Ghosts We Carry," and his reminder that America's roots are more complicated than the Pilgrim narrative, and never separable from race. The intimate dance of identity, a lifelong effort that Grace Talusan, and Kat Geddes chronicle. The sexual and body politics that our "cultural amnesia" keeps us denying, and which we wake up afresh to in the work of, among others, Jennifer Jean and Alexandria Marzano-Lesnevich.

Then there are the pieces that flooded in from artists who felt the same need we did, to confront the impossibilities of our time with work. Brenda Hillman's eye for the incongruous, subtle ways our political realities are personal. Jeanne Dietsch on the effort to reach voters in her rural community. Shanoor Seervai and Elorm Avakame's witness to the experience of national politics as it turns. Kelle Groom's nervous glance at the rising waters. Jaswinder Bolina. Fred Marchant. Robbie Gamble, Bruce Robinson. The graphic storytelling of Lena Merhej and Nick Thorkelson. So many more.

Kim Stafford, who warns us that "When a leader shouts, you have to listen better than he knows how," also gives us the deep wish at the core of Resistance Mic!, and of this Resistance Issue of *Pangyrus*: "When Things Go Wrong, Do Right." People ask me, do you think this makes a difference, this holding of an event in deeply liberal Cambridge, this publishing of a book for the already-concerned? Yes. I do. Because things have gone wrong, and the work of doing right is arduous. It does all the good in the world to be inspired and reminded, restored in your humanity and your hope.

This journal would not be what it is without the inspiration, the unflagging energy, the companionship of my fellow organizers of Resistance Mic!, Timothy Patrick McCarthy and Cynthia Bargar and Sarah Sweeney. Tim's piece here, "May Our Hope Persist," is a love letter to his niece and the beating heart of this volume. He is the best of colleagues, and has done more to preserve my sanity than the rest of the world needs to know. Cynthia Bargar, *Pangyrus's* managing editor and the indispensable managing spirit of Resistance Mic! as well, has taken the journal from an improvisation to an organization, and I am eternally grateful. Sarah Sweeney gave Resistance Mic! its irreverent and bawdy spirit and its inspiration, and some of its most memorable laughs.

A heartfelt thank-you as well to the editors of *Pangyrus*, our copy editors and proofreaders, our sleep-defying designers Abraar Chaudhry and Orpha Rivera, and the many of you who came out to the shows, support the journal, and keep us at this work. "No words," you say? Turn the page. Read them. They are yours.

—Greg Harris

A Can of Pinto Beans

by Robbie Gamble

Just below the ridgeline saddle
tossed to the side of the trail
lying dented among rocks,
bleached label peeled back,
and the downhill-facing end
of the can stabbed through
by some Border Patrol agent's
Ka-Bar knife, a precise wound
mouldering around the edges,
with filaments wafting down
the corners, no, they're streams
of tiny ants, crawling in and out,
bearing flecks of nourishment away.

The Migrants

by Fred Marchant

He hid the fire in a tall hollow stalk of fennel, out of the sight of the great one who delights in thunder. —Hesiod, Works and Days

In those mountains he met others walking in the same direction. Backpacks, black plastic garbage bags, food sacks, a girl with two hard-boiled eggs, the shells flaking off. Some wore t-shirts from the sports teams of the West, and one man still carried an orange life jacket. The hunted, wayward god stood beside a mother who held her infant before her the same way he held the stalk that carried the embers he had stolen. He noted dry myrtle along the side of the road, and saw a ground that seemed soft enough for them to sleep on. There would be at least this much tonight, twigs for a fire, perhaps water for tea, some warmth in the morning.

Pornograph, with Americana

by Jaswinder Bolina

Don't move to Calgary, Apna,
have sex! possibly even with me
if you're willing, not even in wedlock,
possibly backwards with one knee
on the vanity, the shower heaving
steam to the Big Band webcast
out of KCEA, Atherton, my mother
napping downstairs in the great room,
she won't know you scaled the carport,
ducked an eave with a joint and a sixer
of Stroh's, my kurta in ribbons,
your lengha undone, I put every part
of you inside my mouth and bite down
a little as if I'm a rototiller in heat,
you the agitated earth, and I love you,
honest injun! while the sun slinks
behind the Fitch's Big Boy across
the interstate, fireflies make erratic
synapses above the drainage ditches,
the fir trees sway like frat boys
at a kegger, and the neighbors
who watch us framed in the naked
window, who wish us deported
into a darker corner of the duplex,
they can clench their hymnals, Apna,
and glare, we won't go anywhere
Waheguru! Waheguru! we won't go.

Rubble Causeway, Rubble Clinic

by Jaswinder Bolina

Shatter temple, splinter soup kitchen, incarcerate
        the beat reporters and abolish the council, desecrate
        the mosque and dispatch the mayor, you can't delete
        the city. The people are still there shielding their tweens

on buses with their grilles kicked in, the tweens are still there
        blinking at you, every bell there still, and desolate
        the skate park, desolate the market, desolate
        our CorningWare crusted con chutney, avec sofrito

and fish sauce stagnant in the washbasins, so you can cleanse
        all the ethnics, expel every interloper, and cordon the border,
        but you can't scrub the city, its pipework of phlegm, its hair knot
        of telecom cables, subway rave of rats and the last of us

sheltering underground, though come, all you autocrats coiffed,
        you silken thugs, come, all you hard men in loafers,
        root out the last of us, leave her body for the crows,
        but the morgue is still there with its bone show.

Everywhere our graffiti sings. Chlorinate the hood
    and napalm the precinct, you can't incinerate the city,
    our mercury stashed in your groundwater, dioxides
    stowed in your jet stream, the crust and mantel

remember you can't eradicate the city, our broadcasts already
    transmitted, they radio our swelter into the cosmos,
    so the cosmos remembers our traffic and weather together,
    our news on the hour, sports on the 4s, the pitchmen pimping

0% down on all living and dining room furniture, and the living
    remember dining, furniture, napping in flats to the shush
    of tires, billow of curtains, tangle of limbs, somehow
    the sirens always receding, somehow the baby still breathing.

Supremacy

by Jaswinder Bolina

Diodes of the cable modem haunt
the walls a watercolor now I lie awake

and listen for the grope of the king
tide tickling every jetty, for jitters

in the Nikkei Index on the other side
of night, for the boy matriculating now

into a gunman in his efficiency
apartment a couple school districts over,

the barrel bombs thumping Aleppo
while I listen, too, for the rustle

and grunt of the nationalist fitful
in the dank heat of his bedsheets,

the xenophobe fretful I'm somewhere
near, honing my chopsticks, loading

my tortas, my name writ in Gurmukhi,
he fidgets wakeful, fearful I'm awake also

reciting a scripture ruthless as his is,
and I am. I am awake and singing.

Answering Alternative Facts With Fiction
by Maisie Wiltshire-Gordon

*A*t a rally for his tax plan this winter, President Trump gave a stirring description of the legislation's historical significance. It would be "the biggest tax cut in the history of our country," Trump announced. "For years, they haven't been able to get tax cuts. Many, many years since Reagan."

For anyone who remembered the Clinton, Bush, and Obama presidencies, though, his claim was an obvious falsehood. There have been nine major tax cuts since Reagan, and by any of the Treasury Department metrics the Trump legislation falls far short of the all-time top position. As a share of the economy, for instance, it comes in 12th.

But such an easily-falsifiable claim is hardly an anomaly for this administration. Perhaps the most memorable example comes from the first week of Trump's presidency. Sean Spicer, in his debut press briefing, pronounced the inauguration crowd "the largest audience to ever witness an inauguration—period—both in person and around the globe."

Of course, metro data and side-by-side photos made it clear

that this was simply not the case. A few days later on *Meet the Press*, Trump advisor Kellyanne Conway faced a follow-up question: why did the press secretary give false information? "Don't be so overly dramatic," Conway responded. "Sean Spicer gave alternative facts."

The backlash was immediate: "Alternative facts are lies," columnists proclaimed. But in the months since, it has become clear that this was not an isolated incident. Again and again, we find ourselves disagreeing on easily-checked facts. Evidence and research fail to persuade; our usual modes of verification no longer lead to the consensus we'd expect.

Of course, sometimes the truth is hard to get at. Research studies are not always reproducible, and the way experts collect data plays an important role in the trends they uncover. But the "alternative facts" we've seen recently do not reinterpret complicated data sets or bring new information to light. They make claims without offering any evidence at all.

It's not a new political phenomenon. But it *has* become particularly acute—and particularly paralyzing. If evidence does not matter to our arguments, ordinary methods of debate and conversation fall flat. We have lost common ground. How do we build policy when we disagree on reality? How do we respond to the fictions in "alternative facts," when facts themselves seem ineffectual?

I argue it's through fiction even more blatant: literature itself.

I recognize that this may not seem like the most helpful suggestion. "I'm sure literature is very valuable," one of you will say. "Part of what makes us human, and all that. But I don't have time for *Anna Karenina* right now. There are *real-life* trains that are going to hurt *real-life* people if we don't pass some infrastructure legislation."

"And as for *fiction*," another of you will continue, "At the moment I'm pretty focused on figuring out what's true and what's not. Fiction is the one place that *doesn't* need my attention, because it announces flat-out: *This did not happen.* I appreciate the label! But I need to spend my time sorting out the things that don't have labels yet."

But that label is literature's very strength. In this world where facts are uncertain, we have found a single point of agreement. Fiction did not happen, and everyone knows it: Mrs. Dalloway never lived, Hamlet never died, and you will not find Sherlock Holmes on Baker Street.

Fiction is a chance to take a breath from our disagreements about what did and didn't happen. At last, some common ground! We are looking at the same narrative, and we agree on its factual status—in other words, that it is *not* factual. Of course we'll all respond to that narrative differently, and we'll all bring our different perspectives and experiences to bear. But a novel gives us two definitive points of commonality: first, that these are the words we're reading; and second, that they are fiction.

Perhaps this does not seem like much. But when you consider the situation in which we find ourselves—unable to agree on basic facts about how the world actually is—such agreement is significant, and potent.

Reading together is a way for us to see together. The author gives us a perspective: we cannot see the world she has created except through the eyes she gives us. We cannot look to the right unless she looks to the right; we cannot check under the bed unless she says that we will. Fiction requires that we all inhabit the same way of seeing: noticing the same things (because we can notice nothing else); moving the same direction (because it is the author who directs).

Authors help us speak together, too. In the same way that I returned from a trip to North Carolina saying "y'all" and "crawfish," when we read fiction, we pick up on the way characters describe their world. Holden Caulfield's profanity-laced diatribes, the rhythms of Janie's storytelling in *Their Eyes Were Watching God*— these are languages that we learn as we read. When we spend time with a character, we start to absorb her particular way of speaking; we start to see with his particular lens on the world.

In our political realm, we're not there yet. We are having profound trouble learning each other's ways of talking and ways of seeing. But fiction is a start. We may find each others' lenses to be opaque, but perhaps we can see together if we look through the eyes of Holden or Janie.

But does seeing together really make a difference? After all, there's plenty to dispute in fiction: just look at banned book lists or local fights over the 9th grade English curriculum. Agreeing that Colonel Aureliano Buendía is not a real person does not free us from myriad other divergent beliefs.

Sometimes our disagreements are relatively straightforward: "This language is offensive" or "This content is too graphic for teenagers." But often the critique goes deeper. "The author ignores the harm that comes from a unionized workforce," we might say; or "This novel gives a troubling portrayal of women as one-dimensional and without agency." As we read literature, we find that we evaluate even as we engage.

To say "fiction isn't true" then, seems to miss something important about the works we're reading. Our varied responses suggest that fiction actually does make truth claims of some kind. We must think there's something that's *trying* to be true in literature for us to bother disputing it. What kind of truth is it, exactly? Some philosophers say that instead of teaching us *that* or *how*, literature makes a claim about *what something is like*. Others argue literature doesn't posit anything new, but rather reorients us toward knowledge we already have: we recognize its significance; we consider its implications.

But this is an open question, and a difficult one. I only bring it up because it *comes* up: sometimes we read a book and say, "This doesn't feel true," and we mean it separate from the obvious sense in which none of this actually happened. Fiction seemed like the one safe place, didn't it? And yet here we are talking about what's true and what's not.

But at least when we discuss a novel—when we argue about how it portrays women, and if we *like* how it portrays women—at least we are talking about the same novel. At least we are working from the same text; at least we have looked through the same eyes. Fiction does not protect us from disagreement. But it does help inhabit other perspectives. And even if those perspectives do not supplant our own, we have seen with them, we have shared them, we have learned from them.

Fiction helps us build empathy. I don't argue that this is *all* it does, or even the most important thing that it does. But we find ourselves at a bizarre impasse, unable to agree on anything—and fiction gives us a productive way to move forward. We need a point of connection, and we need to get better at making connections. Literature gives us a place to start.

Of course, this is the long game. Books take time to read, and empathy is not a one-click purchase. Fiction lets us engage with one another. But how do we engage with "alternative facts" themselves? Can literature help us find anything to say?

As always, when we hear claims of fact, it is crucial to test them—to look for relevant evidence and consult with experts; to try to understand how the world actually is. But fiction teaches us that if the claim is false, we must not walk away. It is worth paying attention to things that did not happen, and literature helps us understand what kind of attention to give.

The invitation, then, is to read political fiction as we might read literary fiction. What do we see when we look at the world in this way? What is the story you're telling, when you describe the inauguration crowd as the biggest in history? We don't learn *facts* from Trump's comment about the tax plan. But fiction has taught us how to see what a narrator sees without confusing it with what is actually there. Together with Romeo we notice Juliet across the room, even as we recognize that there is no room and there is no Juliet. We feel what it is like to catch Juliet's eye; we understand the kind of person Romeo is to respond as he does. Likewise, together with Donald Trump we look at the tax legislation and feel what it is like to call it the largest ever; we feel what it is like to *want* to call it the largest ever.

Fiction is not a waste of time: there is something to see beyond determining whether these events happened or not. When the claim is that they did take place, by all means press on their veracity: question and cross-reference; validate or invalidate. But if they indeed prove to be fiction, do not give up on them. Pay attention to the narrative that these "alternative facts" are constructing. Consider the values and self-image that they imply. Listen with empathy for the characters in that world, their desires and beliefs, the themes that resonate.

And then invite them to join your book club.

Wake-Up Call

by Jeanne Dietsch

"Any story with robots in it is automatically science fiction," I remember my writing teacher telling me.

I wonder what he would have called a story in which Russian Twitterbots dismantle the US government, and a quarter million women in pink knit caps storm Washington in protest.

I'm something of an expert in robots, it happens, and during the election in 2016 I was writing the final paragraph of my final column on autonomous vehicles for *Robotics and Automation* magazine. "Manual control at the local level, within the robotic vehicle, is critical." I typed. "Passengers must be able to take control, in case of system failure or hostile takeover."

It was a warning call to the thousands of eager young roboticists, men mostly, whose fingers tapped at keyboards around the world, writing the code that will one day control our intelligent transportation systems. Would they even notice my message? Fight to keep manual override, against the pressures of money and the arrogance of thinking we could design perfect systems?

It was my last column because, in part, I'd woken to how our democracy, which I'd long assumed was on auto-pilot, needed manual effort, too. This was why, after a career as CEO of a robotics company, I was devoting my retirement to running for office.

After I hit 'send' on my column, I headed over to campaign HQ—the guest suite over our garage.

"Hey," Steve greeted me as I climbed the stairs. He was in his early thirties, slender and brilliant, polite in a controlled way that's ideal in a campaign manager. "I've got your door addresses and map all printed for you."

"Can't we download them to my phone?"

"They're there, but this is in case you lose cell."

Steve was right, of course. Mountains, even small ones like Pack, Temple and Monadnock, make for spotty coverage, broken connections.

I'm sure my colleagues in tech wondered, though few ever asked, why someone like me lives in a remote village in New Hampshire instead of Boston or the Valley. Would they understand if I told them I get a dopamine rush from being outdoors, from walking to the tiny grocery where the owner greets me by name and knows that I only buy fish the first day it's delivered? Where the wealthiest family in town and families in subsidized housing share the same street? It's an America where people still interact because of common geography. It's a community.

But for how long? It's one of the concerns that had me heading out to my car to spend hours knocking doors.

* * *

Canvassing, especially plugging for yourself, is stressful. Skype, Instagram and texting cannot compare with knocking at the door of someone's home. You're trespassing on their territory. They may be in the middle of a phone call, carrying in groceries, watching TV or playing with children. Not infrequently, they open the door expecting a friend, a repairman or a delivery. Instead, there you are, your badge and clipboard signaling that you're here to talk, to ask questions, to learn about them. Some eagerly share their frustrations. Some stare silently. Still others fume.

Nor can you expect to make sense of the lives you glimpse. A young woman I met the day of my final column was eager to talk. Her low-income housing project was fully visible from the highway. Ancient vehicles listed in the project's semi-circle of tarmac; narrow blocks of struggling grass tiled the area between buildings.

My list of doors included almost a dozen likely primary voters in this complex. I was pleased; that meant the residents realized that who represents them matters.

The young woman lived in the basement level. She buzzed me in.

As I walked downstairs between bare cement walls, a dog began barking. Fortunately, it was not from my voter's apartment, but from another of the three hollow-core doors that faced the basement landing. At the bottom of the stairs, on my left, stood a sandy-haired woman in her twenties in the open doorway.

"Come in, come in! I just got your postcard! I'm going to vote for you!"

I could see behind her a studio apartment, perhaps 300 square feet, dimly lit by ground-level windows on the far side. On the dresser beside the open door, indeed, lay a postcard with my photo. My campaign had mailed these out earlier that week. The tiny apartment walls were bare white except for a poster on the far side. The t-shirted resident's lips were moving, but the dog next door was barking so loudly I could not make out what she was saying.

"He does that all day," she repeated loudly. "I didn't realize until I moved here that people just go away and leave their dogs all day long. People really shouldn't do that to their animals."

She had actually offered to her neighbors to keep the dog, so he would stop barking, she explained. But it had not worked out and they took the dog back. The dog seemed to hear her concern and quieted for a moment.

Before the barking resumed, I asked my standard canvassing question: "Which issues are top of mind for you this year?"

"Mass transit," she replied immediately. "I need a way to get to my appointments."

Transportation was a major issue for many poor people in our rural district, but mass transit? I asked, over the barking, if she used the ride-share program, or any of the church groups that offered drivers.

"It's hard to find someone who goes at the right time," she shouted, "so I usually ride my bike, except in winter I have to walk."

I shouted back I couldn't promise bus service—we weren't big enough to even have Uber--but I would be happy to help her contact a church where members might drive her.

The young woman seemed reluctant. "Well, right now I just want to get my Christmas presents wrapped." I must have looked startled. It was July. She quickly explained, "I like to have plenty of time to enjoy the holiday."

Our conversation appeared to have ended—I, at least, was at a loss for words--so I said good-bye and stepped back up the stairs.

Lives may be unique, but themes, and needs, emerge, when you glimpse into enough of them. One was the urgent need to do something about opioid addiction. We have some of the highest rates in the nation. The fact is difficult to reconcile with the beauty of the pine forests, hills and lakes that surrounded our towns. And the fact that at one time our state was a leader in mental-health treatment.

But then legislators slashed funding for mental health, the university system, schools, roads and just about every other investment in our children's future. Now, our state college's tuition and our graduates' debt ranks highest in the nation. Little research drives less innovation, so the exciting, high-paying jobs grow elsewhere. Meanwhile, the legislature lets minimum wage default to the federal rate, far too low for the area. It is a recipe guaranteed to drive out young people seeking opportunity, and to lead those who remain to seek escape in drugs.

Not that consensus is easy to come by on what to do about it.

Near the high school, grey and white vinyl-sided townhomes stood in trim, well-maintained rows along parking lots. Though it was mid-afternoon on a weekday, at the first door on my list, a young couple answered. Sure enough, their top issue was opioid addiction.

"Why?" I asked.

"We have so many friends who are addicted," the tousle-haired redhead replied. She looked to be in her early twenties, dressed in jeans and t-shirt.

"And the treatment is useless," added the tall, black man beside her. He was about the same age. "They just keep giving them methadone; they don't even try to cure them."

"Well, what should they do?" I asked.

"They have to make them work, get them jobs and get them off drugs altogether," he replied.

They locked the door and headed for their car; I trod a few yards north to the next stop on my phone. The resident, a well-dressed, middle-aged woman, was just starting down the front steps. I introduced myself, handed her a door hanger and asked her chief concerns.

The attractively made-up brunette looked at me and replied without a pause, "Opioid addiction."

I was startled to hear this twice within minutes. My eyes widened even more when she explained that she and her husband led a recovery group for addicts, which was due to meet shortly. I nodded.

"I'm a former addict," she told me. "And my husband is still in recovery."

She continued on down the walk to her car as I stared. How many others, seemingly ordinary people, were in the same predicament, but you never knew until you met them at their doors?

The next time I encountered someone involved with the opioid problem, she had just arrived home. She cracked the screen door, still dressed for work.

"Oh, I thought you were the UPS man."

"Sorry. I'm running for State Senate, so I'm visiting voters in the district to introduce myself."

"I don't have time to talk," the all-business, well-coifed blonde replied, starting to close the door.

By now, I'd learned to just keep talking. "I'm asking people whether any issues are bothering them these days."

"You bet there're issues!" she cried hotly, swinging the door back wide. "These addicts! I work in ER, and they expect us and the police to take care of these people. We already have full-time jobs! They can't dump these people on *us!*"

"What should happen?" I asked, to mollify her.

"I don't know, but it's not us!" She ignored the literature I was offering. "I've had it!" She closed the door definitively, though with not quite a slam.

"Treatment doesn't help most drug addicts," a rehabilitation therapist told me later. It was another sweltering day. We stood at the door of her townhome in the secluded end of a riverside development. Her door was surrounded by flowering bushes and vines.

"I've worked in drug rehab for decades. The state just keeps them for 28 days, then dumps them onto the street. I've seen women walk out the door after a month of detox and shoot up. They meet their dealer on the sidewalk, right in front of the center. Treatment's a waste of time unless you couple it with some kind of 12-step program after they finish."

The opioid crisis showed in nearly every life, sometimes in oblique ways.

One address seemed to be under construction. It was an old white farmhouse, but some of the sills supported brand-new windows, their labels still on. The rooms along the front of the rambling building looked empty, but cars were parked around back. I turned down the drive to investigate and spied a small outbuilding.

A woman answered my knock quickly. She stepped outside to talk, pulling the screen door firmly closed behind her. She welcomed me, but seemed to want to steer me away from the makeshift structure. Beyond the screen I glimpsed an enormous expanse of pale skin, a shirtless man big as a Sumo wrestler. His head gleamed as bare as his enormous naked belly, which he held in place with a wide, leather belt. To the woman's consternation, he began opening the screen door. I saw his looming body press forward and his hand reach out toward me. Then I realized that he just wanted me to take a CD he was holding.

"Listen and learn," he intoned, as I accepted the hard plastic case. He turned back toward his seat inside the small room.

I looked at the CD in my hand. On it was scrawled in indelible marker, "What If Cannabis Cures Cancer?"

"We met on the Internet," the thin, middle- aged brunette was relating as she led me back down the drive. "I moved here from down South and it was love at first sight: in love with him and in love with New Hampshire!"

My eyes took in her sincere, not unattractive face. She explained to me how they wanted to live free from government, but the government was turning the farmhouse into a drug rehabilitation center. They would soon have to move.

Then came the sunny afternoon in the most remote of the 14 towns in our 75-mile-wide snake of a gerrymandered district. My phone was not connecting to cell, but GPS still tracked me as I moved along the country road to the farmhouse listed on my print-out. Cramped from driving, I parked at the beginning of the long stone drive. That way I could stretch my legs a little.

So far that day, few people had been home, so I was pleased to see two women in stretch pants beyond the end of the drive. They were talking in a garden of tall gardenias and roses beside a walk-way that led to the side door.

I strode their way, smiling, in my campaign clothes, clipboard in arm. The rose's scent perfumed my path. The sandy-haired wom-an nearer to the house glanced up and noticed me.

She shook her head and spoke, "It's not a good time."

"Oh, I'm sorry," I replied, hoping to get a few words in, even though she was busy in conversation with her friend. "I'm running for State Senate and just wanted…"

"My son died this morning."

I stopped mid-stride. "What happened?"

"He killed himself." She said it as if she needed to tell it, to spill her anguish across the ground, down the driveway.

I felt her sorrow hit my chest. I was backing up. "I'm so sor-ry. So sorry…" I didn't dare ask further, but I wondered, as I got back in my car, whether the tragedy she was facing might have been connected to the opioid crisis, too. Studies have linked opioid addiction to the rising suicide rates plaguing the young and mid-dle-aged.

Mahatma Gandhi's adage, "Your values become your destiny," was very much on my mind as I drove away. What actions have led to the terrible problems plaguing this state and this nation?

I came to a single story cottage where an elderly, retired school-teacher let me in. I admired the house's straight walls, carefully painted surfaces, sturdy cabinets, level ceiling and perfectly hung, striped wallpaper.

"I did this myself when I was younger," she said, proudly. "I hired contractors to pour the foundation and frame, then once they finished, I built the rest, from the roof down." I pictured her as she must have been, a young woman, strong and determined.

The hardest part had been raising the money. She loved her job as a public-school teacher. But, of course, she did not earn enough to pay all the costs outright, even doing most of the work herself. She applied for loans at several banks. As was common in the mid-20th Century, her application was turned down because she was a woman. Finally, her father loaned her enough so that she could build the shell. She paid for and finished the interior as her earnings allowed.

"But soon I'll have to move," she sighed. The state legislature had raided the New Hampshire teacher's pension fund back in 2010, claiming the recession required it. Meanwhile, almost every year then and since, they cut state business taxes and downshifted more costs to municipalities. As a result, the town raised her property taxes.

This is how it goes. Aging and ill, on a fixed income, she was, at the end of life as in her prime, enduring the consequences a funding formula for schools in New Hampshire that puts 80% of the costs onto local communities rather than sharing them across the state. This means that wealthy seacoast, residents pay lower total property taxes on their million-dollar mansions than she pays for her 3-room cottage. Are these our values? The rich get more, while putting in less, and the poor get less, while putting in more?

There are robots in this story, but it is not science fiction.

On November 8, 2016, voters handed over control of the vehicle of State. They didn't like where we were headed, so they just threw up their hands and let a bot- chorus that amplified their complaints take the wheel.

Unfortunately, this is not a good program for America.

There's a National Public Radio website that hosts a faked video of Barack Obama. In it, he appears to claim he was mistaken when he stated, "There are no red states and no blue states, only the United States." He says, in the video, that his most important role right now is to play golf. An inset simultaneously reveals the actor whose face and voice are manipulating the visage and speech of our former President. It's a software app.

When trust is at its lowest, in case of system failure or hostile takeover, manual control at the local level is critical. Passengers must be able to re-take control of the vehicle.

This election, we're building our canvassing team early. We'll be knocking on a dozen thousand doors, speaking face-to-face to tens of thousands of voters. I can envision us and those like us, simultaneously knocking, all across the nation. Women, mostly, of all races. Our necks crane forward, eyes intent on the eyes we meet, building the connections that will network the American people, town by town, state by state, to steer our country's future.

Trump's Executive Order Attacks the America I Know and Love

by Shanoor Seervai

*I*n this moment, America is not mine. It cannot be—it is not like anything I have seen.

I came here in 2007, one year before Barack Obama was elected our president. *Our* president, because America was mine then. Not mine in passport—I'm an Indian citizen—but in what I believe is worth fighting for: that everyone, regardless of their gender or color or nationality, has a right to be here and wake up in the morning and work toward a better and more just future.

I came here when I was 18, just as my adult life began, before I was tethered to a single way of being. So I became the version of hybrid Indian and American that I was before the election, that I will continue being. But President Donald Trump and his administration are snatching that out from under my feet.

Trump's first move was to close the border to refugees and issue a 90-day ban on anyone entering the United States from seven predominantly Muslim countries. The list of countries has not expanded to India, and is unlikely to; I'm aware that the persecution many immigrants and foreigners are facing is far more acute than the distress I am feeling. Yet if you ask one non-citizen to leave, you're signaling all of us to be prepared. You're telling us we aren't welcome, that we do not belong.

I can't contemplate leaving. This is my home. Then I wonder how to stay and witness this ugliness, this spiral away from everything America stands for.

The day after the ban was signed, Harvard University emailed me, warning: "all foreign nationals should carefully assess whether it is worth the risk to travel outside the country." A risk to travel outside the country? I am on the sixth U.S. visa I've held in the last two decades—I've never before been told that traveling on a valid, legitimately obtained visa to a democratic country could be a risk.

This warning distresses me, not because of my own immigration status, but for the fragility of the future it portends.

I am still in Cambridge, Massachusetts, but my heart is breaking for all the people who are stuck at borders, at airports, in camps. Federal courts granted emergency stays--but nothing reversed the ban. And the mean-spirited nativism remains, and is still spreading across the country like wildfire.

My heart is breaking, because to turn our backs on refugees is to deny some of the world's most vulnerable people the support of the world's most powerful country. Much of my research as a graduate student has been about the refugee crisis, about how countries from Germany to Jordan to Sweden are responding to the desperate plea from Syrians fleeing the civil war in their home. America is responding differently.

"It's only seven countries," a friend's classmate said. Seven countries, but all it takes is one act of filtration, seven nationalities not-good-enough to send the dominoes cascading.

The pillars of American openness and decency in which many have long held faith are shaking, shaking from side to side my confidence that this country could belong to me. Shaking my conviction that when I knocked door to door in New Hampshire to talk to voters, I was doing it for our collective future. I have a stake in America's future. I want a stake in America's future. I care about this country. But maybe when I wake up tomorrow the headlines will say something different.

Everyone asks what I am doing, what they could do, what we should do, and I have no answer. I can't even read the news. Protest? Yes. Sign petitions? Yes. Donate? Yes. Call our representatives? Yes. Lobby Congress? Yes. But then what? Watch helplessly as the edifice of a tolerant and inclusive America crumbles?

I have no answer, but the demonstrations in cities and towns across the U.S. and the globe, offer some reassurance that we haven't rolled over in acceptance. This is not normal, it never will be, and we need to summon the stamina to resist, today, tomorrow, every day.

This piece was first published on January 30, 2017. President Trump since announced two updated versions of the executive order. The Supreme Court upheld the third ban in June 2018, ruling that Trump's decision to ban or restrict travel and immigration from seven countries, most of them majority-Muslim, was within his constitutional authority.

The author has since moved to Brooklyn, New York, on her seventh U.S. visa.

Eyewitness

by Seno Gumira Ajidarma

Translated by Jan Lingard

The eyewitness entered. He had no eyes. Unsteadily he made his way through the courtroom, groping the air with his hands. Blood ran from his eye-sockets, blood so red it seemed nothing could be redder than the red of that blood, flowing slowly and continuously from the holes where his eyes had been.

The blood soaked his cheeks, soaked his shirt, soaked his trousers and soaked his shoes. It oozed over the floor of the courtroom, which had just been mopped; the smell of disinfectant still lingered. The courtroom was in an uproar, the spectators' cries revealing their emotion. The journalists, responding as always to sensational events with great excitement, enthusiastically began photographing the eyewitness from all angles, even from upside down, heating up the atmosphere even further with the blinking of their camera flashes.

"Outrageous!"

"Insane!"

"Sadistic!"

His Honor the Judge quickly sized up the situation and pounded his gavel. With the remnants of his authority he attempted to restore order. "Silence ladies and gentleman! Be quiet! Anyone who disturbs the proceedings of this court will be removed from the courtroom."

The spectators quieted down. They too were anxious to find out as soon as possible what had really happened. "Eyewitness."

"Yes sir."

"Where are your eyes?"

"Someone took them sir."

"Took them?"

"Yes sir."

"Do you mean you had an operation?"

"No sir, they were scooped out with a spoon."

"What? Scooped out with a spoon? Why?"

"I don't know why sir but they said they were going to make curry soup with them."

"Make soup? That's outrageous! Who said that?"

"The people who took my eyes, sir."

"I know that, you idiot! I mean who did it?"

"They didn't tell me their names."

"Didn't you ask them, stupid?"

"No sir."

"Listen carefully you fool, I mean, what did they look like? Before they were scooped out with a spoon, allegedly to make curry or maybe goat soup, your eyes were still in your head weren't they?"

"Yes sir."

"So you saw what they looked like, didn't you?"

"Yes sir."

"Why don't you tell the court what you saw with your eyes

that have now probably been eaten by those curried soup fanciers."

The eyewitness was silent a moment. All the visitors in the courtroom held their breath. "There were several of them sir."

"How many?"

"Five sir."

"What did they look like?"

"I didn't get a chance to look closely. After all, they did it so quickly."

"Do you still remember what they were wearing perhaps?"

"I'm sure they were wearing uniforms sir."

The courtroom erupted again, like the buzzing of a thousand bees. The judge pounded his gavel and the buzzing stopped. "Do you mean army uniforms?"

"No sir."

"Police?"

"No, it wasn't police."

"Civil security men perhaps?"

"You know what I mean sir, they were all in black, like in the movies."

"Were their faces covered?"

"Yes. Only their eyes were showing."

"Ahaa, I've got it! They were ninjas weren't they?"

"That's it sir, they were ninjas! That's who scooped out my eyes with a spoon!"

Once again the spectators became rowdy and chattered to each other as though they were in a coffee stall and once again His Honor the Judge had to pound his gavel so everyone would be quiet. Blood still trickled slowly but continuously from the black eye-sockets of the eyewitness, who was standing like a statue in the courtroom. The blood ran over the floor that had just been mopped with disinfectant. It filled the courtroom and then overflowed out through the door and down the steps to the yard. But nobody saw it.

"Eyewitness."

"Yes sir."

"Tell me, why didn't you call for help when your eyes were scooped out?"

"There were five of them sir."

"Couldn't you have screamed, or thrown something? Surely you could've done something so your neighbors would hear and help. Isn't your house in a slum where you can hear the people across the alley even if they're only whispering? Why did you keep quiet?"

"Well you see... because it happened in a dream sir."

Everyone burst out laughing and again the judge pounded his gavel angrily. "Silence! This is a courtroom, not a circus!"

The courtroom was stifling. People were sweating profusely but they didn't want to budge. The blood in the yard flowed out to the car park. The judge continued his question. "You said just now it happened in a dream. Do you mean it was so fast it was like a dream?"

"No sir, it wasn't like a dream, it really must have been a dream, and that's why I was quiet when they went to spoon out my eyes."

"Don't play games with me. Remember you have to swear this under oath later."

"I'm deadly serious sir. I didn't call out because I thought it was just a dream. I even laughed when they said they wanted to use my eyes to make curry soup."

"So according to you, the entire eye-scooping episode only happened in a dream."

"Not just according to me sir, it really must have happened in a dream."

"You could, of course, be crazy!"

"But here's the evidence it was a dream sir: Ask anybody, all around. They'll all testify that I slept all night and nobody disturbed me."

"So it definitely happened in a dream, did it?"

"Yes sir."

"But when you woke up your eyes were gone?"

"That's right sir. That's what I can't understand. It happened in a dream but when I woke up it turned out to be true."

The judge shook his head, quite perplexed. "Ridiculous," he mumbled. The flowing blood had reached the main road. Could an eyewitness without any eyes still be a witness? Of course he could, thought His Honor the Judge. His memory wasn't carried off with his eyes, now was it? "Eyewitness."

"Yes sir."

"Can you still testify?"

"I'm ready sir. That's the reason I came to this court first instead of going to the eye doctor."

"Do you still remember everything that happened, even though you've no longer got any eyes?"

"I do sir."

"Do you still remember how the massacre occurred?"

"Yes sir."

"Do you still remember how they fired wildly and people toppled like felled banana palms?"

"Yes sir."

"Do you still remember how blood flowed, and people moaned and those who were still half alive were stabbed to death?"

"I do sir."

"Remember it all well, because although there were many eyewitnesses, not one of them is prepared to testify in court except you."

"Yes sir."

"Once again, are you still willing to testify?"

"I am sir."

"Why?"

"For the sake of justice and truth sir."

There was pandemonium in the courtroom. Everyone applauded, including the Prosecutor and Defense lawyer. Many people cheered, and a few of them even started chanting slogans. His Honor immediately rapped his magic gavel. "Shh! Don't you campaign here!" he said firmly. "Today's hearing is adjourned and will resume tomorrow to hear the testimony of the eyewitness who no longer has any eyes."

With his remaining energy he once again pounded the gavel, but it broke. Everyone laughed. The journalists, who were forced to write about minor news items because they weren't free to report major stories, quickly took photographs. Click-click-click-click! His Honor the Judge was captured for posterity holding his broken gavel.

On the way home His Honor said to his driver, "Imagine a person having to lose his eyes for the sake of justice and truth. Shouldn't I, as a servant of the law, make an even greater sacrifice?"

The driver wanted to reply with something that would dispel his guilty feelings, such as, "Justice is not blind", but the judge had fallen asleep in the annoying traffic jam. The blood still flowed slowly but surely along the highway until the city was flooded. It wet every corner of the city, even creeping over multi-storied buildings, until there wasn't one place that was free of the blood. But miraculously, not one person saw it.

When it was night the eyewitness who no longer had any eyes said his prayers before he went to bed. He prayed that life in this world would be just fine, that everything would run smoothly and everyone would be happy. In his sleep he had another dream. Five men in ninja uniforms tore out his tongue, this time using pincers.

1-800-HOT-CHAT

by Jennifer Jean

It's such a dumb thing small thing. Right? I'm on the phone faking this guy out. Maybe some regular. He can't know that I pick toe jam out my toenails in this warehouse with maroon cubicles with soft grannies & few students in swivel chairs. He's just one more dumb small dud buying. Not touching. Just phone fucking me from a BBQ. Okay. It's June outside. "What's cooking?" I ask hungry. "Halibut," he laughs, "What's cooking with you?" I look around at the stale air. I've been losing weight the wrong way lately — without money. On my way in on my bike I saw a crowd at the bus stop & maybe no food made me think they swayed over some lady flat on her back on the sidewalk. Her fat feet in beige pumps stuck out over the curb. "That food sounds good. You should get some," I say picking fresh pimples & blotting puss with my sleeve. "Forget that," he says & we chat about what we'd do but like kids do: "Let's pretend you do this. & then I do that." Okay. Sometimes it doesn't work like when kids say, "You're dead!" & you say, "No I'm not!" But who decides? & this is what I want to know when I start hearing the BBQ. Kids closing in. Kids fading like running around.

I hear a woman's question. "Flowers," she says. There's his muffling hand his slick whisper like a shrug or dad or door clicking. Then nothing. "Oooo-kaaaay," he says like he's my boyfriend's pal Trey who tells everyone I call him—chat hot when I don't. Would never. He's all "Oooo-kaaaay" the way he wasn't with Ms. Flowers. & I drop the receiver. Stop my desktop solitaire game. 'Cause I'm sick & froze & there's a kind of life behind his voice. & it's touching me.

An excerpt from "Defenses"
by Krysten Hill

I.
They follow me out the bar.
Want an apology for the untouched drink
they sent over. It's funny that I won't
turn around or slow down, that my flight
gives me away. That they can put my name
and shape it any way in their mouths.
They catch it with the phlegm in their throats
and spit it on the sidewalk.
Because every man is the one
who took me into a room and wouldn't let me out,
I carry a pocket knife. Palm it on my way home.
Even for the man I love,
there is a knife inside my nightstand.
Because *a bitch can't say thank you,*
a rock catches up to my heel
and I am down on the ground.
They laugh at the noise I make when I fall,
the animal that comes out of a wilderness in me.
They back away with their hands up
because it's a joke after all, and to prove it,
one tries to help me off the ground. I reach out
and slit another laughing mouth
into his hand.

II.
In the writing workshop, he asks:

Is there any way
you can write this poem
from his perspective?

III.
My mama never taught me to fight
not because she didn't know
how to turn her own black body
into a baseball bat hiding
behind a bedroom door,
but because she thought that everything
would be different for me.
Could spare me the lesson
of what it was to prepare my body
for a war I was already standing in.

Among Some Anapests at Civic Center

by Brenda Hillman

(including a line by Tobias Meneley)

The fascists have entered the town

      Sun like a late   ripe peach

City says no
to masks

We go with the crows & the crowd
      A defensive line is made

My telomeres   all lined up

The State prepares the tear gas canisters
      (almost wrote teenage canisters)

My pronoun is wearing a mask
A defensive line is made

We go with the G & the H

Poets are often tired
We don't think the hitting will work
We grow calm   among the zeroes

My house was a little too calm
        Our telomeres all lined up

i'm too old to jump over walls

A terrible beauty is dead

& the sun was tender upon us

i don't think the hitting will work
A defensive time is made

A poem is not a protest

The Nazis have entered the park

Subject to history's impress

My telomeres all lined up—
        Subject to cosmic rays

Aw Aw awe awe crows say

My house was a little too calm
Was thinking of Nicolás Guillén

Was thinking of William Blake

We go with the crows & the crowd
Hate hate hate hate free speech

i'm too old to jump over walls

A defensive line is made
      Subject to history's impress

i don't think the hitting will work

Changed utterly wrote Yeats

Sun like a late   ripe peace

The State unfolds the tear gas thermoses
We follow the crows   Awe Aw

A defensive line is made
A defensive line is made
My house was a little too calm
A defensive line is made
i follow the crows & the qualm

repeat repeat repeat

Civilization

by Stephanie Burt

October 2017

as in Boston
as what it looks like
when you leave it

taking off
your undercoat
of smog

as if from inside
the gumball machine
at the top of the old
control tower at Logan

from when we built airports
and thought they could stay
half the globe away
the President expostulates and is

no longer followed by
his opposite number his doom
his ghost his
Little Rocket Man

I'm not the man you think
I am at home
I am not he

nonetheless I wish to leave
this message for
civilization thanks
for everything

for feijoas also known
as pineapple guavas
multiple names
for all the best things

for César Franck's violin
sonata for fanfiction for
the next
generation (literally the kids)

where nobody should have
to start from scratch
to start over

as if coming from
deep space anyway *it feels
like we almost made it*
as one later singer

managed to say
even if
we are not
going to be okay

May Our Hope Persist:
A Love Letter for My Niece
by Timothy Patrick McCarthy

America, June 2018

Dear Malia,

Let me begin with what matters most: *I love you.*

I don't know how many times I have written this letter in my mind, and I have no idea when you will read it. It started as soon as you were born. I was the fifth person in our family to hold you. I'd never before met a human that new to the world. You were very small, but you weighed *everything*. I can't forget the look on the nurse's face when she came into that hospital room in Boston and saw you in my arms as you settled into your first night's sleep. Not everyone can see what is so obvious to us: we are *family*.

You look very much like your folks. You have your father's eyes and your mother's smile, both of which are excellent things, because Mommy and Daddy are Black and beautiful and brilliant, like you. You also have their spirit, their *essence*, which is at least as important, because the truth is that you were born into a world that too often measures human value by the surface of things rather than the depths—the skin, not the *soul*. This is terrible, of course, but it is also treacherous for a child like you, born at the intersection of so many things this country seeks to covet and control, and deny and destroy. We will teach you all this history someday—soon—before this reality becomes too obtrusive and the nation's relationship to you becomes too abusive. And it most certainly will, given its long criminal record. I hope you will always know that we have tried to love and protect you—fiercely, ferociously—since before you even knew us.

I have known your father since he was even younger than you are now. We met when I taught at his elementary school, when he asked me to be his brother, when Auntie and Nana welcomed me in, when we all first fell in love. Ours is an uncommon story, a really beautiful one: we are a *chosen* family. There are other family stories that are not mine to tell. Yours is a complex inheritance, but one thing is constant: we are not *fancy* people. We have had to make our way in this world, too often with undeserved difficulty, against overwhelming odds, but we persist, on our strongest days, like the superheroes you love to read about in books. Let me say this about your father, my brother: he is a very good man, tough and sensitive in equal measure. He is named for his father, a man broken by an unjust war and his own very bad demons; because of these things, you will never know him. But Daddy is still a dreamer, a man of peace who loves hard and refuses to break, as much as this nation conspires to guarantee it. Many thousands before him have gone another way, including some of our childhood friends—mine as well as his—but he has taken a different road, with no guarantees but the ragged, resilient hope that offers a fixed, flickering beacon in the tougher times.

You, on the other hand—*you* were named for the eldest daughter of Barack Hussein Obama. Yours was a very popular name back then, that historic year when he became the First Black President. That was a really big deal, though it feels like a lifetime ago. When I think of how young you still are, I have difficulty apprehending how much has changed in such a short time. I'm an historian, which means that I tell stories about people from the past as a way to make sense of whether things change over time; put another way, I track this nation's progress so we can hold it to account. I am afraid that when the stories are told of *that* time—the moment of your precious birth into this nation—it will be seen not as an acceleration point for justice, as many of us hoped and expected, but as a break-ing point when the arc of history got bent backwards, again. I want to be wrong, for the sake of your entire generation, but I feel it in my bones that we've been here before. After all, your Mommy and Daddy and Uncles and Aunties—*we* are all from a different time; and your ancestors—well, *they* were born into harsher circumstanc-es than most of us have had to endure. We all wish for progress, some of us have felt it and many of us work hard for it, but we must never *expect* it. I had fallen in love with the fantasy that you would be much older before you figured out that a mediocre white man— much less a madman who hates families like ours—could run the country. But history has a peculiar, stubborn way of being repeti-tive, which is why I was so relieved, and inspired, when you said to me recently: "He is everything you teach me not to be." How I wish you could vote.

America intended for you and me to be enemies. You can't yet fully comprehend this, thank God, but this country was built, in large part, to keep people like us apart. The colors of our skin— yours black, mine white—are falsified fragments of evidence that have long been used as fictional alibis to justify and pardon some of the worst crimes against humanity. You may not remember this, but several Christmases ago you asked Daddy: "why isn't Uncle Black?" We all made a joke of it at the time—you know how we like to laugh about these things at home—but the deeper meaning was clear: *why am I not like you?* It's a good question, impossible for me to answer. But when that older white boy called you that racist slur on that school bus in elementary school, I wanted so badly to change the color of my skin, to be as Black as you and Daddy and Mommy and most everyone else in our family, or to have none of this matter any more. But these, too, are fictional fantasies, because race and racism have always been the realest things about America—the wretched foundation of its original sins, the rotten core of our ongoing inheritances. After all these years, I don't know which is my bigger fear: that you will someday see me as an adversary, or merely an exception. But my *biggest* fear is that the people who look an awful lot like me will someday break your spirit—force you to doubt yourself, or worse, convince you to participate in your own undoing—because *this* would finally break my heart. To prevent that, you must discover your own truth, never let anyone unmoor it, and cling to it as if your life depends on it. *Because it does*. Please keep this wisdom from the great ancestor James Baldwin close to you: "Take no one's word for anything, including mine, but trust your experience. Know whence you came. If you know whence you came, there is really no limit to where you can go. The details and symbols of your life have been deliberately constructed to make you believe what white people say about you. Please try to remember that what they believe, as well as what they do and cause you to endure, does not testify to your inferiority, but to their inhumanity and fear." You seem to already know this, somehow, because you asked us this about that white boy: *why is he so angry?* That really is the *essential* question.

Whenever I worry about you, and we do, I try to remember all the times *you* have shown *us* what it means to be free. When you didn't bat an eye the first time you realized that CJ and me—your Black Uncle and your white Uncle—have been married to each other almost as long as you've been alive. When you came to your birthday party one weekend in camouflage and cornrows and my birthday party another weekend in twists and a pink superhero tee. When you warned me, with a serious smile, that I would need to learn how to twist and braid before you'd ever let me do your hair. When you announced that you want to be a boxer and an astronaut and the President of the United States, and saw nothing unreasonable with any of this. *Because there isn't.* When you told the little boys on your basketball team to pass you the ball because the team has a better chance of winning if they do. When you began your training in martial arts because you want to protect yourself and never hurt others. When you changed from the bright colors we suggested to a black blazer of your own choosing before you introduced yourself to the real life superhero John Lewis. When you pay no mind any time someone insists that you "eat like a girl," or shrug your shoulders any time someone complains that you "act like a boy," and just carry on whenever someone says you're either "too sensitive" or "too tough." When you tell us how much you love Janelle Monae, and we aren't the least bit surprised. Perhaps all of this stems from the fact that you were born into a family that is Black and interracial and Queer and feminist and so many other perfectly wonderful things. Perhaps it's because you're being raised by a vast village of tough women and sensitive men. Perhaps you are just who you are—strong and happy, a *new normal* beyond the old boundaries—and that, my dear, is just fine. You write your own rules, play your own game, and live (and love) on your own terms, because this, at last, is what it means to be free.

I would be a fool to promise you freedom. Ours is not a world where such promises are usually kept. And in any case, no one can give another person freedom. We must find it for ourselves, and too many people never do. That doesn't mean you have to search for it alone; history teaches us, many times over, that there's strength in numbers. *And there is.* There will be struggles ahead, for sure. This nation will impose its unfair burdens upon you, and disappoint you more times than you will be able to count, but you can't let any of this *break* you. Our promise to you, *all* kids like you, is this: as you find your own freedom and live your own truth, we will continue to love and protect you—fiercely, ferociously, *fabulously.* We will get up each day, for as long as we are able, and tear down, as best we can, the obstacles in your way so that *you* can light and lead the way to a different world.

You recently gave me a birthday present: a small bracelet with shiny round beads, a purple tassel, and four black and white dice that spell H-O-P-E. You told me you were giving me hope because I give you hope. The world will always need hope, Malia, because hope is the root and the wellspring of freedom. May we always find it to give. *I love you.*

Your uncle,
Tim

Incantation

by Czeslaw Milosz, 1968
trans. the author and Robert Pinsky

Human reason is beautiful and invincible.
No bars, no barbed wire, no pulping of books,
No sentence of banishment can prevail against it.
It establishes the universal ideas in language,
And guides our hand so we write Truth and Justice
With capital letters, lie and oppression with small.
It puts what should be above things as they are,
It is an enemy of despair and a friend of hope.
It does not know Jew from Greek or slave from master,
Giving us the estate of the world to manage.
It saves austere and transparent phrases
From the filthy discord of tortured words.
It says that everything is new under the sun,
Opens the congealed fist of the past.
Beautiful and very young are Philo-Sophia
And poetry, her ally in the service of the good.
As late as yesterday Nature celebrated their birth,
The news was brought to the mountains by a unicorn and an echo,
Their friendship will be glorious, their time has no limit,
Their enemies have delivered themselves to destruction.

Poem of Disconnected Parts
by Robert Pinsky

At Robben Island the political prisoners studied.
They coined the motto *Each one Teach one*.

In Argentina the torturers demanded the prisoners
Address them always as *"Profesor."*

Many of my friends are moved by guilt, but I
Am a creature of shame, I am ashamed to say.

Culture the lock, culture the key. Imagination
That calls boiled sheep heads "Smileys."

The first year at Guantánamo, Abdul Rahim Dost
Incised his Pashto poems into styrofoam cups.

"The Sangomo says in our Zulu culture we do not
Worship our ancestors: we consult them."

Becky is abandoned in 1902 and Rose dies giving
Birth in 1924 and Sylvia falls in 1951.

Still falling still dying still abandoned in 2005
Still nothing finished among the descendants.

I support the War, says the comic, it's just the Troops
I'm against: can't stand those Young People.

Proud of the fallen, proud of her son the bomber.
Ashamed of the government. Skeptical.

After the Klansman was found Not Guilty one juror
Said she just couldn't vote to convict a pastor.

Who do you write for? I write for dead people:
For Emily Dickinson, for my grandfather.

"The Ancestors say the problem with your Knees
Began in your Feet. It could move up your Back."

But later the Americans gave Dost not only paper
And pen but books. Hemingway, Dickens.

Old Aegyptius said Whoever has called this Assembly,
For whatever reason—it is a good in itself.

O thirsty shades who regard the offering, O stained
earth.
There are many fake Sangomos. This one is real.

Coloured prisoners got different meals and could wear
Long pants and underwear, Blacks got only shorts.

No he says he cannot regret the three years in prison:
Otherwise he would not have written those poems.

I have a small-town mind. Like the Greeks and Trojans.
Shame. Pride. Importance of looking bad or good.

Did he see anything like the prisoner on a leash? Yes,

In Afghanistan. In Guantánamo he was isolated.

Our enemies "disassemble" says the President.
Not that anyone at all couldn't mis-speak.

The *profesores* created nicknames for torture devices:
The Airplane. The Frog. Burping the Baby.

Not that those who behead the helpless in the name
Of God or tradition don't also write poetry.

Guilts, metaphors, traditions. Hunger strikes.
Culture the penalty. Culture the escape.

What could your children boast about you? What
Will your father say, down among the shades?

The Sangomo told Marvin, *"You are crushed by some
Weight. Only your own Ancestors can help you."*

Mixed Chorus

by Robert Pinsky

My real name is Israel Beilin. My father
Was a Roman slave who gained his freedom.
I was first named Ralph Waldo Ellison but
I changed it to the name of one of your cities
Because I was born a Jew in Byelorussia.
I sit with Shakespeare and he winces not.
My other name is Flaccus. I wrote an essay
On the theme You Choose Your Ancestors.
It won't be any feeble, conventional wings
I'll rise on—not I, born of poor parents. Look:
My ankles are changed already, new white feathers
Are sprouting on my shoulders: these are my wings.
Across the color line I summon Aurelius
And Aristotle: threading through Philistine
And Amalekite they come, all graciously
And without condescension. I took the name
Irving or Caesar or Creole Jack. Some day they'll
Study me in Hungary, Newark and L.A., so
Spare me your needless tribute. Spare me the red
Hideousness of Georgia. I wrote your White
Christmas for you. And my third name, Burghardt,
Is Dutch: for all you know I am related to
Spinoza, Walcott, Pissarro—and in fact my
Grandfather Burghardt's first name was Othello.

Sic Semper Tyrannis

by Sebastian Johnson

"The struggle of man against power is the struggle of memory against forgetting."
— Milan Kundera

I. Invention

One of the first documentations of African people in British North America dates to 1619, when approximately 20 captives from present-day Angola disembarked at Jamestown. Slavery as an institution did not yet exist in Virginia, but it was widespread in practice. The form was the indentured servitude of some English colonists by the ruling elite. These indentured servants worked four to seven year terms, and could be bought, sold or traded. They could be mistreated, even killed, at will. And since the mortality rate in early Jamestown exceeded 50 percent, indentured servitude was a life sentence in most cases.

Historian Barbara Fields, in her foundational work "Slavery, Race and Ideology in the United States of America," identifies the economic and social concerns that created the need for black settlers to been seen as a race apart. Improving mortality rates made life-long enslavement a financially lucrative possibility. Furthermore, African settlers existed outside the common English cultural and social considerations that governed interactions between the classes. Colonial elites could subjugate Africans without fear of dampening further immigration and settlement.

Events soon took a turn that made racial difference an ideological imperative. In 1676, armed rebellion broke out in Virginia against the colonial government. White and black indentured servants joined arms together against the elite. Though the rebellion was crushed, officials recognized the danger posed by the disaffected. Through piecemeal efforts, the rights of African servants were curtailed. Slavery became a legal category separate from servitude. The law established that children born to enslaved women would also be enslaved. Intermarriage between black and white colonists was forbidden. And by the beginning of the 18th century the first slave codes in America were codified.

At the center of our national myth is the story of Plymouth Colony, Massachusetts, where English pilgrims and native tribes forged early alliances. In many history books, Thanksgiving is a tidy precursor to the American Revolution, which arose in the same colony and cements our vision of ourselves as fighters for freedom and lovers of liberty.

But despite the focus on Massachusetts, no state boasts a better claim to being America's birthplace than Virginia. It was in Jamestown that leaders first made white supremacy a matter of public policy. Leaders in Virginia promulgated the racial caste system that softened class divisions and made possible the notion of an egalitarian, free white society. Virginians reconciled the notion of universal equality with the persistence of chattel slavery. And it was in Jamestown that the logic of white supremacy was hitched to global capitalism through plantation agriculture. Massachusetts birthed the revolution. But Virginia, mother of presidents, sired America.

And no place, having done so much to bring America into existence, did as much to threaten its demise in defense of white supremacy. Virginia's entry into the Confederacy elevated the cause of secession to a contest for the nation's soul, given the state's strategic, economic and symbolic significance. Virginia served as the Confederacy's capital and furnished many of its greatest military leaders. John Wilkes Booth, who assassinated Lincoln, is said to have screamed the state's motto – "*Sic semper tyrannis*," or "Thus always to tyrants" – before making his escape.

White supremacy, as both an organizing principle and foundational creed, has been an integral part of our history and identity. As Fields maintains:

During the revolutionary era, people who favored slavery and people who opposed it collaborated in identifying the racial incapacity of Afro-Americans as the explanation for enslavement. American racial ideology is as original an invention of the Founders as is the United States itself. Those holding liberty to be inalienable and holding Afro-Americans as slaves were bound to end by holding race to be a self-evident truth.

Of course, a house divided cannot stand. The paradox of unfreedom in the land of the free was ultimately resolved in bloody conflict. But the ideology of white racial superiority born of the paradox has remained with us, performing a similar function – the concealment of injustice in biological determinism.

II. Subversion

The efficacy of white supremacy is never as apparent as when the concept itself is under threat. An obscure episode in Virginia history illustrates this truth.

In the 1880s, during the dying embers of Reconstruction, a biracial, populist movement briefly seized control of Virginia state politics. Led by a former Confederate general, the Readjuster Party was born in opposition to paying back the ruinous state debt incurred during the Civil War. Elites had voted for war, the Readjusters reasoned, and now the elite expected to be repaid for the cost. The party argued forcefully that state revenues should go to public education – crucially, they argued that this education should extend to all Virginians, black and white. The party gained power with considerable black support; 26 black state legislators caucused with the Readjusters or were elected on their party line. The *Richmond Dispatch* marveled that the Readjusters were "the first party organized in Virginia since the war which has broken color line."

The ambitious program that the Readjusters began included "the repudiation of state debt, the abolition of the poll tax, extensive investments in public education that doubled the number of schools, teachers, and students, as well as the creation of Virginia State University," the first fully state-supported university for black Americans.

A similar coalition, the Fusionists, would be formed across the border in North Carolina. Between 1894 and 1900, poor white farmers and black Republicans worked in tandem to elect joint candidates and implement favorable policies. Fusionist officeholders, a significant number of them black, liberalized access to the ballot box and increased taxes for education.

But just as quickly as it began, the cooperationist movement dwindled in the face of resurgent racial animosity. The banning of the whipping post and the high visibility of black faces in state government provoked backlash. In 1883, a race riot left five dead in Danville, Virginia. The riot gave ammunition to conservative defenders of the old order, and their preferred candidates swept the legislature. The Readjusters were soon a distant memory. In North Carolina, a constitutional amendment to limit black citizens' access to the ballot passed in 1900, ending the Fusionist movement.

There were further populist uprisings in the South throughout the 1890s, led by men like "Pitchfork Ben" Tillman, that represented the class interests of poor white Americans. But these movements either ignored the racism of the time or used it as a wedge. In the end, the missed opportunity for solidarity was to the benefit of the old elites, who eventually reasserted their authority.

III. Lessons

The election of Donald Trump, a demagogue riding populist anger and nativist fears, has historical precedence. He is the latest in a long line of opportunists – from Strom Thurmond and Louise Day Hicks to Joe Arapaio and Steve King – to spin white *ressentiment* into electoral gold.

Yet Trump's antecedents do little to lessen the shock of his ascension to the Oval Office through foreign manipulation and suppression of the vote. Many are grieving today because their belief in their country has been shattered.

Americans are an ahistorical people. This trait has fueled our disdain for the storied pomp of ancient lands, made us a magnet for those seeking to escape the constraints of the past, and established us as a mecca for innovation and reinvention. It has also blinded us to the realities of our nature as a people; caused us to see crisis where we should see continuity; encouraged us to prefer the cozy familiarity of national myth to the starkness of truth.

Many believed that the fact of President Obama would be enough to transcend our bitter history. The fact of President Trump now serves as a grotesque correction, but we should resist the urge to over-correct. Progress is not inevitable, but then neither is retrenchment.

The grim (or hopeful) reality is that we live in the country we have always lived in, and we continue to be ourselves, for better and worse. Throughout our history, some Americans have sought to dominate and rule through fear and hatred. Other Americans have fought back, have insisted on the bedrock decency of our values, have dreamt what never was and willed it into being. There will be no escaping the long arm of white supremacy, but resistance is just as vital a part of our birthright.

At even the lowest point of our history, as the promise of Reconstruction congealed into Jim Crow, former slaves and former Confederate soldiers built political power together in service of a shared agenda. It was not because the erstwhile rebels had purged their individual hearts of prejudice; and indeed, the moment was short-lived. It was because, like the Pennsylvania couple in 2008 who "voted for the nigger," the hope of solidarity outweighed the psychic comfort of imagined superiority.

It was because Americans of goodwill and long perspective were willing to continue organizing and fighting for our values despite the vagaries of the political climate and an atmosphere of despair. Our challenge is to be like those Americans — to be unyielding in defense of our progress, yet gentle with one another. To bear the burden of a long, twilight struggle against the disease of racism in the heart of our body politic. To confront the contradictions of Whitman's multitudes in the service of true freedom.

Donald Trump swept every state of the former Confederacy last November, save one: Virginia. Mother of presidents. Prodigal daughter. Thus always.

A Declaration: Forbidding Mourning
by Bruce Robinson

This is a time we'd like to forget
a virulent inflection that pains and yet
cannot last unless we let it,

This is the way it flows, a liquid
breaching of the brain, merest trickle
at first, until a torrent looks to save us,

This is what we learned, what we surmised:
not alone the languished fabrics, but the
dyed, the raw sensation washed and wise,

This is a siren sent to persuade us,
this over-promised (ever promising)
and under-delivered indignation.

from The Lost Family

by Jenna Blum

As part of *Resistance Mic!* Jenna Blum read this excerpt from *The Lost Family*, her novel centering on Peter Rashkin: a German-Jewish Holocaust survivor who survives Theresienstatdt and Auschwitz, emigrates to New York, and remarries--only to find that he, his American wife, and their daughter are haunted by the young family he lost during the war. In this scene, Peter is responding to his American cousin Sol's question about why Peter didn't get his first wife and their twin daughters out of Nazi Germany while there was still time.

"So you deny it? You deny that you and your friends—Choppers, Dutch, that doctor, the suppliers—you deny you're connected?"

"Sure we're connected," said Sol. "But not the way you think. Not Kosher Nostra—like Meyer Lansky and Bugsy Siegel and those guys. We're just a buncha guys who came up together, like I told you. We're not mobsters. We don't get involved with drugs and gambling and whores—we leave that meshuggaas to the Italians. We're numbers guys. The worst we do is maybe massage the numbers a little."

"To buy arms. And make a nice profit from it, too."

Sol reared back and glared at Peter, his eyes watering behind his glasses.

"We don't see profit," he said. "Whaddaya take me for? We're not criminals. We give back. I give back to the guys by giving them business, they help me raise money, every cent goes to defense. To protect our people over there."

"It's for war," said Peter. "And let me ask you something. These people you raise the money *from*, the people I *helped* you get money from, do they know what it's going for? Guns and tanks and planes?"

Sol shrugged. "A couple do. Most don't. But that's all right. We give some money to the up-front causes too. Hospitals. Orphanages. The Joint. Red Cross. We just stretch the contributions a little, creatively, to cover defense too."

Peter sat back. All the catering he had done for Sol's luncheons and dinners and brunches, in the law firm, in homes all over Manhattan and Westchester and New Jersey. All the years Peter had been the poster boy for Sol's good causes. How many darkened rooms had Peter sat in, while Sol clicked off slide after slide of emaciated Jewish children, of the melee in the DP camps, of trawlers full of survivors, bound for Palestine but sunk by the British before they could get there? Of men and women gazing out from bunks, skeletal, in rags, toothless, each bearing a tattoo like Peter's own? "We gotta help 'em," said Sol as people wept softly in the dark—by no means all women. "We gotta help our own. They survived Hitler's filthy camps—for what? To return to homes burned to the ground. To go back to shtetls that no longer exist. They want to come to this country—but there are quotas, waiting lines; our government says there's no room, sorry, we can't take 'em. Well, I'll take 'em," said Sol, "and with your help I'll make sure they'll all get here safe. Like this guy here," and he would gesture to Peter with his slide-show clicker, Peter who had been standing next to the podium in the dark, now stepping into the bright beam of the projector, rolling up his shirtsleeve to show his tattoo.

"I'm done," Peter said. "I'm through being your shill."

"Fine with me, Mr. Conscientious Objector," said Sol, relighting his cigar. "Guys like you, you sit around thinking about right and wrong, hold hands, sing 'Kumbaya,' and then when somebody's burning your house down, you say, 'Help! Help!' Before the war, when we were sounding the alarm, trying to get people out, you guys said, 'Nah, you're exaggerating, sit tight, it'll blow over.' Until they started herding you into the camps, and then who'd you turn to? The dirty-money guys. You think the world should be all flowers and sunshine, and maybe it should, that's nice. But the world doesn't work that way."

"You sound like my father," said Peter.

"Good," said Sol. "Now there was a smart man. A fighter. Willing to put his mouth and his money on the line. If it weren't for him, there'd be a lot more dead Jews. If you'd been more like him—"

"—I'd be dead too," said Peter. "The Nazis would have dragged me off to Buchenwald too, and there'd be no one left."

"They hauled you off anyway," said Sol. "And you barely made it. Haven't you wised up by now? You of all people, I'd have thought you'd learned a lesson over there."

"My lesson?" Peter spat. He was so angry his lips were numb. "Don't you talk about my *lesson*. It is *not* the same—Israel and Germany. You have no idea what it was like. No idea at all. Don't you understand, we'd lived in Berlin for a *century*. It was our city—the way New York is yours. Germany our country. And then some strutting idiot, this little fool, this bigoted madman screaming idiocies with spit flying from his mouth—he comes in telling lies. Oh my God, the lies! The lies, the lies, the ridiculous lies. We never heard such stupid things. Every day a new one—our mouths were hanging open. We Jews had collapsed the economy—it wasn't the Versailles Treaty, oh no. We were bankrupting Germany. We had a Jewish master plan. Also—my favorite—he said we had declared war on Germany. War! We had! While our rights were being taken away from us one by one, first the movies and then parks and our pets and jobs and even riding on streetcars. *We* were undermining Germany. *We* were winning. Who could believe it? Who could believe such black-is-white horseshit? We laughed; we thought sooner or later people must wake up and say, 'All right, enough is enough, the emperor has no clothes,' and send him on his way. We never thought he'd stay. That things would get *worse*. We never thought that our friends—my parents' friends, the people we worked with, educated, civilized, cultured people, good people, people who *knew* right from wrong—we never believed they'd believe him. Or pretend they did, which was the same thing. Don't you see? There was no precedent. It was unbelievable that anyone could believe such lies lies lies lies lies!"

Peter stopped for breath, aware that at some point he'd jumped to his feet, that he had been shouting, that the people on line at Walter's were looking at him. Sol was considering the end of his cigar.

"Of course there was precedent," he said calmly. "What the hell are you talking about?"

"People've always wanted to kill us," said Sol. "Cossacks. Pogroms. Nazis. Arabs. The uniforms change, that's all." He pitched the cigar stub toward the gutter. "Precedent or not, who cares? That's the trouble with you guys. Always thinking about ideas, when what matters is what's actually happening. Use your eyes. Use your ears. If you'd done that back in Germany—"

"Don't say it!" Peter shouted.

"—your family might be alive today," said Sol.

Peter's whole body clenched—and then all the fight went out of him. He felt very tired. He looked over at Walter's, at the people waiting on line for hot dogs; at the tiny leaves, just born, fluttering in the breeze above him; at the new daffodils and tulips springing from the mud; at the big American cars whooshing past on Palmer Avenue. Sol could talk all he wanted about how the world worked, but he was an American, and he would never know what it was like, how dumbfounding, how confusing, how paralyzing it was when it all went wrong, when the place you'd lived in your whole life, your city, your beloved country, abruptly and for no reason except the rants of a rabid fool, turned against you; when the place where you got your morning coffee and roll and had your hair cut and smiled good-morning to the neighbors as they walked their dogs—when that place started ejecting you. Suddenly you were invisible, and the next day worse: you were despised, you were filthy, you were vermin, and you stared in astonishment at the erosion of your life, no more films, no more work, no freedom of movement, no citizenry, no home, and by the time your mind caught up with events, it was too late, and your government, friends, and neighbors were joyously hunting you down like dogs.

"I want out," Peter said. "I won't bankroll war. Any war."

Sol shrugged. "Suit yourself. You want out, you're out. But if you're too good to help me, you're too good for my money. You're on your own. Don't come to me with your hand out."

"I won't," said Peter. "I'm done with that."

"You sure?" said Sol. "I'd think about it if I were you. Without my money, you'll be outta business by the end of the year. Nothing personal. Just numbers."

"I'll take the chance," said Peter. "I'd rather live on food stamps."

Sol planted his hands on his knees and pushed himself up. "Okay, big talker," he said. "I'll give you a week to think about it.

Because you're family." He hitched up his pants. "You might be fine eating government cheese," he said, "but that fancy piece you've been shtupping, something tells me she won't be so happy with it. How long you think she's gonna stick around when you're living under some bridge like a schvantz?" And off he stomped to his car.

IN 2005, COMING FROM BEIRUT, WHERE THE INTERNET IS VERY SLOW, I CAME TO GIVE AN ANIMATION WORKSHOP.

I WAS THRILLED TO SEE HOW PROGRESSIVE THINGS WERE AND EXITED PEOPLE WERE ABOUT NEW TECHNOLOGIES.

AFTER ALL, I SAID TO MYSELF I WAS IN UMM EL DUNIA, THE MOTHER OF THE WORD : EGYPT!

AND SO DESPITE THE EXTREEME POVERTY, THE OBSCENE DEPRIVATION AND THE OBVIOUS OPPRESSIONS, SOME YOUNG WOMEN AND MEN I MET DURING THE ARAB DIGITAL EXPRESSION CAMP TAUGHT ME ABOUT THE STRUGGLE THAT WAS YET TO COME.

MANAL AND ALAA: A LOVE STORY

LENA MERHEJ

THEY MET DURING A COMPUTER CAMP IN EGYPT AL NOSOOR AND HAVE BEEN INSEPERABLE EVER SINCE. MANAL WAS TWELVE AND ALAA WAS THIRTEEN

SINCE THEN, THEY WENT ALL OVER GIVING WORKSHOPS ON BLOGGING AND VOICING OUT ONE'S OPINION ONLINE

ON THE 7th OF MAY 2006

11 BLOGGERS WERE THROWN IN JAIL...

FOR PARTICIPATING IN A PEACEFUL PROTEST IN SOLIDARITY WITH EGYPT'S FREE JUDICIARY MOVEMENT.

"... I HAVE TO DEFEND KEFAYA* AND ALL THE DIFFERENT MOVEMENTS, I HAVE TO EXPLAIN ABOUT THE JUDGES. AND I HAVE TO EXPLAIN WHY I AM HERE, WHY IT'S WORTH IT, AND TO BE FRANK I'VE NO IDEA WHY. IS IT WORTH BEING AWAY FROM MANAL FOR THREE DAYS LET ALONE 30 (MASHY YA MASR) BUT I CAN'T REALLY SAY THAT CAN I?"

*KEFAYA ("ENOUGH" IS THE EGYPTIAN MOVEMENT FOR CHANGE)

"WE'VE NEVER BEEN SEPERATED FOR MORE THAN A WEEK. I'M NOT USED TO THIS. IT'S THE FIRST TIME HE'S BEEN AWAY FROM HIS TWO LOVES: ME AND HIS COMPUTER"

"TODAY IT HIT ME, I AM REALLY IN PRISON."

2003: AGAINST THE INVASION OF IRAK
2004: AGAINST THE MUBARAK GOVERNMENT
2004-2010: 300 LABOUR PROTESTS

WHEN ALAA WAS OUT, THE WORKSHOPS CONTINUED.

MANY NEW BLOGGERS BECAME INVOLVED IN REPORTING NEWS ABOUT THE PROTESTS.

WHILE OTHERS CREATED A CULTURAL UPRISE WITH NOVELS, FILMS AND MUSIC.

MANY BLOGGERS WERE THROWN IN JAIL OVER AND OVER, STRUGGLING WITH THEIR FREEDOM TO EXPRESS CURRENT OPPRESSIONS AND CORRUPTIONS

MANAL AND ALAA'S LOVE KEPT STRONG

"DEEP IN LOVE IN A MOST SUBTLE/ORGANIC FASHION."

"WE CHANGE, YES. WE GROW, YES... BUT IN THE SAME DIRECTION... WE GET CLOSER."

"HOW WONDERFUL LIFE IS WHILE YOU'RE IN THE WORLD..."

"MY FAVORITE SPOT ON EARTH, WITH MY FAVORITE PERSON IN THE UNIVERSE..."

MANAL AND ALAA BOTH COME FROM FAMILIES OF POLITICAL AND HUMAN RIGHTS ACTIVITY.

IN THE EARLY EIGHTIES, ALAA'S FATHER, AHMAD SEIF AL ISLAM HAMAD WAS IN PRISON FOR FIVE YEARS FOR INVOLVEMENT WITH A COMMUNIST GROUP.

بلادي بلادي بلادي

* NATIONAL ANTHEM

FROM WHEN ALAA WAS VERY YOUNG, I HAD TO TELL HIM THINGS LIKE, 'THERE ARE BAD POLICEMEN AND GOOD POLICEMEN'. I HAD TO EXPLAIN THAT PEOPLE CAN GO TO PRISON FOR BEING GOOD, NOT BAD.

"LATEST ESTIMATES AS OF 23/11/11 SUGGEST THAT OVER 30 DEMONSTRATORS HAVE BEEN KILLED BY MILITARY ACTION IN THE LAST FOUR DAYS."

MILITARY VIRGINITY TESTS PERFORMED ON FEMALE DEMONSTRATORS INCLUDED ELECTRIC SHOCK TREATEMENT, BEATING AND RAPE.

ALAA'S MOTHER WENT ON A HUNGER STRIKE WHEN HE WAS AGAIN DETAINED IN OCTOBER 2011 TO FACE CHARGES OF INCITEMENT TO VIOLENCE.

ALAA REFUSES TO BE INTERROGATED BY THE MILITARY PROSECUTION RESPONSIBLE OF THE BLOODY CLASHES IN MASPERO. MONA, ALAA'S SISTER FOUNDS THE "NO MILITARY TRIALS TO CIVILIANS" CAMPAIGN.

"I NEVER EXPECTED TO REPEAT THE EXPERIENCE OF FIVE YEARS AGO. AFTER A REVOLUTION THAT DEPOSED THE TYRANT, I GO BACK TO HIS JAILS?"

"... REJOICE OH MOTHER OF THE MARTYR WE ARE ALL KHALED SAID..."

THE DAY MUBARAK STEPPED DOWN, MANAL AND ALAA FOUND HOPE AND DECIDED TO GET PREGNENT.

"HOW CAN I NOT BE THERE TO SEE HIS FACE WHEN KHALED IS BORN TO SEE HIS MOTHER'S FACE AS SHE SEES HIS FACE?"

River of Grass

by Kelle Groom

For mystery, focus on the wrong thing:
the palm tree instead of the man in black,
the curtain instead of a bird, pinprick eye, head
of tiny dots masked, blame neighbors
and children for not spotting a small darkness
in the corner of sky, ballooning:
we lived in a park with no stores or traffic lights:
we were tranquil and wooded:
flute players join the tubas
lifted to mouths,
drummer hands silent:
the shooter wore a gas mask, had hand grenades
head turned, elbows bent:
listening: curvy ink backs:
pulled the fire alarm:
an AR15 shoots through a body
and through a wall:
through a lookout tower:
at elementary schools:
in the fog skirts flare like a circus:
muzzle easy to control:
the glass shattered one in the head
one in the leg blood on the floor:
I don't want your condolences,
your punching bag, your exclamation marks:
it is too late it is too early
it is too death house it is too lethal current

too dark helmet
it is too autopsy table
too flush up against the screen.

Natalie Said

by Kelle Groom

at MIT they were talking about the flood.
A student said the problem isn't
that our wall is too low,
because no wall
is high enough to save us.
Instead we should become like pearl divers like
mermaids, adapt backwards get gills
prepare
to go back into the water.
It was November in Far Land it was yesterday in the lab,
it was the harbor & light house, but you can barely see it
beyond one boat left under the clouds.
One night in Florida in a classroom
of students preparing to take a test,
I had to know the meaning
of *there* where the real subject
follows the verb: *There is very little time.*
I was nervous I wouldn't be able
to hang on
to what that means.
I have a problem with the early dark, I told Natalie.
Yes, she said, *that's a problem here*. I wondered how cold
drowning would be,
how much would I fight
before I believed I was in bed
blanketed. The problem with believing we need a wall
is the problem of asking the wrong question.

What if everything is the wrong question? The moon
is five days old. *In Alaska the seagulls all live in the trees.*
Natalie's looking for work, she's working for free,
she's been here 17 years, a decade in a barn.
I can't talk to her, I said *there's nothing to hang
onto,* except now, we have mermaids & pearl
divers, & the student from MIT
who is going to Japan
to learn from the Ama, to hold her breath, swim
to the bottom of the sea, who will let out
a long low whistle, & survive.

Practical Water

by Brenda Hillman

What does it mean to live a moral life
It is nearly impossible to think about this

We went down to the creek
The sides were filled
       with tiny watery activities

The mind was split & mended
Each perception divided into more

& there were in the hearts of the water molecules
       little branches perpendicular to thought

Had lobbied the Congress but it was dead
Had written to the Committee on Understanding
Had written to the middle
       middle of the middle
       class but it was drinking
Had voted in cafes with shoplifters &
       beekeepers stirring tea made of water
       hitched to the green arc

An ethics occurs at the edge
of what we know

The creek goes underground about here

The spirits offer us a world of origins
Owl takes its call from the drawer of the sky

Unusually warm global warming day out

A tiny droplet shines
          on a leaf & there your creek is found

It has borrowed something to
          link itself to others

We carry ourselves through the days in code
DNA like Raskolnikov's staircase neither
          good nor bad in itself

Lower frequencies *are* the mind
What happened to the creek
          is what happened
          to the sentence in the twentieth century
It got social underground

You should make yourself uncomfortable
If not you who

Thrush comes out from the cottony
          coyote bush glink-a-glink
                    chunk drink
          trrrrrr
          turns a golden eyebrow to the ground

We run past the plant that smells like taco sauce

Recite words for water
      weeter wader weetar vatn
      watn voda
[insert all languages here]

Poor Rimbaud didn't know how to live
      but knew how to act
Red-legged frog in the pond sounds like him

Uncomfortable & say a spell:
blossom knit & heel affix
fiddle fern in the neck of the sun

It's hard to be water
      to fall from faucets with fangs
      to lie under trawlers as horizons
      but you must

Your species can't say it
You have to do spells & tag them

Uncomfortable & act like you mean it

Go to the world
Where is it
Go there

Triple Moments of Light & Industry

by Brenda Hillman

During our protest at the refineries, our friend R tells us there are bugs in the oil in the earth-colored vats at Valero & Shell, tiny slave bacteria changing sulfides, ammonia, hydrocarbons & phenol into levels of toxin the mixture can tolerate, & then we consider how early tired stars gave way to carbon molecules a short time after the start of time & now carbon makes its way in all life as the present tense makes its way in poetry, the sludge in the vats where the hydrocarbonoclastic bacteria break things down to unending necessities

of   which Dante writes

of   the middle of hell

light   where no light is —

R says his friend who tends the bugs for the company feels tenderly toward his mini-sludge-eaters, they are his animals, he takes their temperature & stirs them & so on. We pause to think of it. Such small creatures. At the beginning of life the cells were anaerobic, ocean vents of fire, archaea, then they loved air. In the axis of time there are triple moments when you look back, forward or in. As a child you were asked to perform more than you could manage. Your need was not symmetrical. It is impossible to repay the laborers who work so hard. R describes his friend's work as devotional. The bacteria do not experience hurt or the void but their service is uneven & that is why i protest.

Home No More

by Boyah Farah

I stood in the fourth-floor lounge at Cambridge Innovation Center, my gaze switching back and forth between the innovators—who were drinking their morning coffees and teas—and the Syrian refugees on the large flat-screen TV. While the news watchers seemed sympathetic, I knew they couldn't begin to understand what was about to happen to those women and men, children and elders.

I was once one of those refugees fleeing the horrors of war. What the images couldn't show—what I shall never forget, for as long as I breathe—is the colossal void that existed in our minds in the camp.

In 1993, I was fifteen years old and confined with my family in the Utanga refugee camp outside of Mombasa, Kenya. Erected in the middle of nowhere, the camp was surrounded by the half-naked women, men, and children of the indigenous Giriama tribe, who often poked their heads out from bamboo huts in the forest. Sitting in front of our tent, I often saw drunken Kenyan men staggering beyond the barbed wire fence where we, along with thirty thousand other refugees, were penned in—prisoners without a crime. We were in someone else's backyard, sitting on someone else's soil, and breathing foreign air. They did not want us around, but we had nowhere else to go because our home, our real home, was no more.

Our three-bedroom house in Mogadishu had been replaced by two tents in the middle of the forest, our bathroom by a forest toilet in the bush, and our kitchen by a leafless acacia tree standing alone in between the tents. The dust field where my childhood friends Hassan and Ali and I used to chase soccer balls under Mogadishu's magnificent blue sky was replaced by brown sand with swirling dried feces. Those games—along with our pigeons, our hens, and our two goats, Bella and Bilan—were now just memories, which I carried carefully because they were all I possessed. In the camp, nothing belonged to us. The world expected us to start our lives from this nothingness.

Since we had lost our country and we added no apparent value to the world, we were held in a pen. Anyone from the outside world could visit us, but we could not leave. Many years later, I still remember the day I walked out of the camp hoping to see what the city of Mombasa was like, only to return to the tent with three scratches zigzagging from my arm to my upper back. One of the drunken security men had hit me as he told me to get back inside. With all that my mother already had to deal with, I felt bad showing her my wounds.

During my year living in the camp, I saw more women, men, and children dying from such mosquito-borne diseases as malaria and dengue than in my last two years in Somalia's vicious civil war. In the tent next to ours, a skeletal man in his thirties coughed, wheezed, and spat gray specks of mucus onto the sand. No one would talk to him; he was isolated until his soul departed. Knowing that I, like everyone else, was waiting to die there, I wished to meet God with a pious heart. But praying had never been my thing, so I struggled to do it. We all had difficulty processing our enormous emptiness, abandonment, and isolation; our desperation meant that anyone with a well-crafted narrative could exploit us for their nefarious political ends.

Bearded Middle Eastern men wearing white ankle-length garments called *Thawb* with religious textbooks tucked under their armpits came and spoke Arabic to the self-appointed religious camp leaders, all of whom were in their twenties and wore scarves coiled around their heads and necks. My friends and I would walk behind these men who were speaking a language we could not understand because it gave us something to do.

We often saw white people, mostly men wearing black suits, white shirts and red ties, stepping out of the white four-wheel-drive trucks with antennas poking upward and bearing the logo of the United Nations High Commissioner for Refugees. They filled our bellies with grain, oil, powdered milk, and occasional spaghetti. And so, food was no longer an issue for us, but our minds remained as empty as the clear sky. Because we were hungry for any purpose beyond the barbed wire, the tents, the feces, smashed Jerrycans, brown mud, the gazes of women, and the drunken Kenyan men, we welcomed the bearded men who helped us set up religious institutions in the camp.

The white men fed our stomachs with rations, but the Middle Eastern men fed our minds with purpose, allowing us mental escape. This was how our Somali clan-infighting metastasized into religious ideological war with global reach. Al-Shabaab, a Somali-born militant group now battling the UN-backed government in Somalia, was partly born out of the refugee camp. Similarly, the camps occupied by Iraqis after the 2003 U.S. invasion gave birth to ISIS, and Afghans in Pakistan's refugee camps produced the Taliban.

One hazy morning, before the sun's rays had lifted to heat the tent, I woke up to chirping birds. Four of my brothers, three male cousins, and four other males—family friends who had grown up with us in Mogadishu—all lay inside the tent with their heads together. Buck-toothed Omar in his twenties was sleeping next to me on the mattress. He was the only one of us who woke up for Morning Prayer. I saw him sitting crossed-legged as he faced east to Mecca with prayer beads in his left hand. He was talking to himself.

Before coming to the camp, Omar had been a Rambo-like fighter who often wore a red cloth wrapped around his forehead and brandished an AK47. He smoked three packs of cigarettes while dipping tobacco beneath his lower lip. He chewed *qat*, a shrub whose leaves contain a compound with effects similar to those of amphetamines. A person chewing it could experience excitement, loss of appetite, and euphoria.

In the camp, Omar often got up and ate two slices of dough with a cup of tea before he walked to the hut to play poker with other men. He smoked cigarette butts he picked up from the ground. He asked other men for a tobacco dip. He scavenged for Qat stems lying in the sand and chewed them. At night, I often saw Omar sneaking out of our tent to go to the hut located down in the dark alley beneath two trees where he would watch porn movies on a battery-powered, nineteen-inch Magnavox television. Two Giriama men ran the camp movie theater where they showed Hollywood and Bollywood movies by day, but skin flicks at night.

One night, I snuck out of the tent and followed him to the theater. Peeking in through the cracks, I saw men's faces in the flashing light from the television as they sat on the sand grunting, whimpering, and squealing in the dark. Unable to buy cigarettes or chew tobacco or Qat, Omar grew quieter, like most of the young men in the camp. In the face of the great void, his dignity withered like a lone dying tree in the forest.

One day, Omar met a Somali man his age, one of those who

wore a Muslim handkerchief coiled around his head. I saw them stroll together in the camp, drink tea, and walk to the hut that served in our section of the camp as a mosque. Within a week, Omar had quit all his bad habits and grown a beard. He carried a twig to brush his teeth five times a day. He cut his pants above his ankles. He lowered his gaze whenever a woman walked nearby. Suddenly, he started to preach against watching indecent Western movies, gambling, smoking cigarettes, and chewing tobacco. Omar was a changed man, and as he walked, the elders sitting outside of the tents, whose heads were bowed and whose hands held sharp stones for removing fleas hidden beneath their toenails, would respectfully greet him, "Salaam." (Removing fleas was a chore that none of us liked, but in the camp, opening your skin with sharp glass or stone to get out the fleas living beneath your toenails was as routine as brushing your teeth).

Beyond the quarrels of the men sitting in their huts, the gazes of boys and girls orphaned and mothers widowed by the civil war, Omar found his escape in the worship of God; but he was not knowledgeable about the scriptures.

One hazy morning, as I saw him talking to himself, I wiggled my body closer and tilted my head toward him to listen. To my teenage mind, Omar—as a fighter, a Qat-chewer, a pornography-watcher, a smoker, and now a pious Muslim—was the epitome of what it meant to be a man.

"If these men kill my father, I will kill one hundred men to avenge his murder," he said speaking to God. "And if you want to, you can throw me into the fangs of hell." Oblivious to my stare, he continued counting prayer beads. "My father is a ninety-year-old innocent man." He paused and murmured, "I will return to Somalia and kill men."

His father was still in Somalia where clan conflict was at its peak, as women, men, and children died for their clan affiliations.

His father, along with other elders, had been captured by the en-
emy clan and his current whereabouts were unknown. As Omar
spoke to God regarding his plan to murder a hundred men, he was
not after the would-be killer or killers of his father but he wanted
to fill the nothingness of his pathetic life in the camp, meaning that
what Omar was really after was purpose, value and history—or
perhaps a group to belong to. The nothingness of our lives was our
number-one enemy.

One morning in the camp, I fetched a bucket of water from
a large yellow Jerrycan, sat in front of the tent, and washed my
hands. I brushed my teeth with a twig I snapped from a tree. From
where she sat behind the stove cooking, steam billowing from her
tea kettle, my mother handed me two slices of dough in a white
ceramic plate and poured me a cup of tea. As I ate, I counted the
trees and watched the sun climb behind the trees and move into the
sky. Midday, as the internal nothingness grew heavy in my mind,
as all sense of purpose seemed cleaved from my head forever, I
got up, put on my rubber flip-flops on, picked up a Jerrycan, and
then walked out to the camp center where the main water-tap was.
Carrying that goddamned yellow Jerrycan to collect water for my
family was the most exciting and meaningful part of my day.

Once I was there, I picked a fight with a boy. As my fist flew
against his torso, he ducked and hit me back in my face. Despite the
blows I received, my predominate feeling was one of hope–albeit
a false hope of subduing my boredom and dispersing the nothing-
ness. If I was not fighting a boy, I would be watching other boys
brawling over nothing. We all felt the same way. We would have
done anything—we would have burned the world; we would have
killed every last soul in it—if it meant we could fill that void that
claimed us all.

When I came to New England from that filthy refugee camp in
Kenya, I was excited about coming to America, but I felt very little

hope about people. It was the two-legged creatures of Bedford High School who first showered their mercies on me. Whether buying for me my first winter jacket and white converse shoes, paying for my education, or even their simple gesture of showing their teeth in welcoming smiles, they showed me that humanity was still intact and that I was part of something larger and more compelling than my experience of war. It is because of their combined efforts that I am now a writer, a speaker and an educator.

War removes mercy. It orbits around the globe like the sun and, God forbid, it might one day hover over this land, too. Empathy builds bonds of mercy. Be kind to the refugee. We are all the same species. In your time of hardship and need, others will return your kindness.

In Search of Tito Freddie

by Grace Talusan

A writer is for liberation.

I learned this from my second cousin, Alfrredo Navarro Salanga, a respected writer in the Philippines. He sent me books he had written and would tuck a letter in the front pages. He encouraged me to read and write as much as possible and to call him Tito Freddie, and think of him as an uncle.

If it wasn't for my maternal grandmother's yearly visits from the Philippines, I could not be certain that such a place actually existed beyond my family's stories. When my lola noticed that I always had a book in front of my face, she told me about her nephew Freddie. He was a prolific writer and could do all kinds: journalism, poetry, fiction, criticism, even plays. You are becoming like him, she told me.

Honestly, I didn't believe my grandmother. I could not conceive of anyone who looked like me as the author of a book. My grandmother was as real as the fairy godmother in Cinderella. She swooped in once a year bringing dried watermelon seeds, milk candies, and stories of this fantasyland called Manila, only to vanish without a trace. We did not call her (too expensive) or write letters (the mail would only get lost in the Philippine postal system).

My grandmother told me to write Tito Freddie a letter and she promised to hand-deliver it to him. So in 1982, at ten years old, I wrote him a letter and forgot about it.

The next year, my grandmother returned with a letter tucked into a softcover book, titled Davao Harvest. The name Alfrredo Navarro Salanga was on the spine. I was amazed. Here was an actual book written by a real writer who was related to me. In my American suburb, I was at the public library every week, but had never encountered a book by a Filipino, much less one related to me. When it came time for my grandmother to return again to the Philippines, I wrote Tito Freddie another letter. I told him how much I loved his book. I was eleven years old. In truth, I had desperately tried to make sense of the dense the literary anthology, but I couldn't do it. So I lied.

By 1983, people in the US had heard of the Philippines because Benigno Aquino Jr., a Newton, Massachusetts resident for three years, had been assassinated. In October of 1984, my grandmother delivered another letter from Tito Freddie, the only one that I still possess, along with In Memoriam: A Poetic Tribute by Five Filipino Poets. Aquino's smiling face was on the cover of the yellow booklet. Tito Freddie wrote:

These poems cost us all a great deal of pain because the people who ordered himkilled don't like the idea of people thinking him a hero. That may sound strange to you but it is true and that is why you should be thankful that you live in a country where you are free – to write about what you want to and to speak out your mind when you want to.

I was not yet a teenager, but old enough to understand the gravity of what he was saying. He picked his words carefully. Until I read that, I didn't realize how powerful I could be as a writer. What kind of responsibility this was. Also, I had never thought of myself as lucky to live in the US, because I had taken my freedom of speech for granted. I felt a great responsibility to use this privilege because there were people in the world who could not.

In the same letter about Aquino, Tito Freddie wrote, "He was a great man who risked his life and lost it so that we Filipinos can be free. We're not free yet but we will be someday and by then I hope you can come over and pay a visit."

I'm sure I wrote back that I'd see him in Manila someday, but I wasn't serious. How could I go somewhere that seemed made-up?

Tito Freddie's bravery and conviction, though, taught me what a writer is for. A writer is for setting words down, one after the other, and through their sentences, freeing the reader from boredom and tyranny, and offering possibility. For penning sentiments like, "We're not free yet but we will be someday." There is hope in the "will be."

I turned thirteen and my grandmother visited again, very excited about my pen pal's recent success. In 1985, the Philippine Jaycees awarded Alfrredo Navarro Salanga the Outstanding Young Men (TOYM) Award for Literature and Journalism.

* * *

I kept my promise to my uncle, eventually. As a grown adult, I returned to the Philippines. My official reason was to work on a research project, but really I wanted to reconnect with the country that I had left as a child. I wondered who I would have become if I'd stayed, what I'd lost by living my life in a different place. And I especially wanted to seek out my pen pal, though it was too late to meet him in person. He had died 27 years before, at the young age of 40.

Once I was in the Philippines, I looked for signs of him in libraries and bookstores, at his alma mater the Ateneo, at his widow Alice's apartment, and finally at his grave. I read his books; I touched his awards; I went through hundreds of pages of correspondence, "Thank You" notes that showed how generous he was with his time and resources; "I'm Sorry" letters from schools in the US that he hoped to either study or teach in, and surprisingly warm requests for payment from a bill collector that became sweeter the more time passed.

An aunt, now also long dead, had once told me that she had read the letters I had written Tito Freddie. "How is that possible?" I'd asked. She said she had seen them on display. At the time I'd been embarrassed that my deepest girlhood yearnings had been exposed. Now I could find no record of that display, or anyone else who had ever heard of my letters--to the point I started to question whether I had even written them. I think this questioning of reality is a psychological tic that was created in me when I left one country and started again in a new one. Much about my early life in the Philippines holds a status between reality and dream.

When I visited Tito Freddie's archive at Ateneo, I read his TOYM acceptance speech and learned about a painful part of his history. In 1976, while Freddie was living in Mindanao, his friend Eman, a writer and activist who joined the New People's Army, was detained. Martial law was in full swing and many thousands of people were detained.

Almost two weeks passed until they heard news. A cemetery worker had seen four bodies hastily buried at the Tagum municipal cemetery in Davao. Freddie accompanied the group of relatives and friends to the site, watching the men dig. Even when they saw the flash of skin against the earth, for a few moments, perhaps they still hoped. Maybe there had been a mistake.

But there was no error. Upon seeing his friend's remains, Freddie's reaction was "near- hysterical tears," recounts Sylvia Mendez Ventura in her essay, "Emmanuel Lacaba: Poet- Warrior." And no wonder. Eman's hands and ankles were bound and "the flesh on his back had been macerated by the rocky terrain over which he had been dragged like a dead cow."

Freddie did not leave Eman until his friend was returned to his family. Eman's brother, Jose F. Lacaba, never forgot what Freddie had done by helping to locate, exhume, and transport the body back to Manila, writing, "I will always be grateful to him for that." As horrific as the sight was of his beloved friend's corpse, Freddie did not look away. He did what writers do. He wrote, bearing witness to Eman and others in his work.

"Journalists nowadays are said to fear for their own lives for doing what they must be about," Freddie said at that awards ceremony. He spoke about Alex Orcullo, a Davao writer who, driving home on his 38th birthday with his wife and young son in the car, was removed from his seat and shot thirteen times in the back. Even on a night when Freddie was being celebrated, he used the moment to tell the truth. As partygoers drank cocktails and shook hands with each other, Freddie named his colleagues, writers who were currently sitting in jail cells because they had criticized the government. He dedicated the award to those in his generation who had been killed or imprisoned because of their beliefs about democracy and free speech. He said, "It is not I alone who walk this stage tonight but they too."

GMA Network journalist Howie Severino remarked that Freddie "was a writer in the worst of times. He had close friends who were killed by the military; he himself was jailed. He knew that he had gifts that had a higher purpose than just fame and fortune. He gave young writers like myself the gift of his example, and the gift of his time and attention. He knew much more than most that we would grow up and develop into people who could make a differ-ence."

Tito Freddie did not just write poems, novels, short stories, and plays, he also wrote newspaper columns and articles. He was imprisoned for several months during martial law for writings crit-ical of the Marcos dictatorship. Thirty years after Freddie gave that speech, the Philippines is still considered a deadly place to practice journalism. We hover at a shamefully low place on the Reporters Without Borders' World Press Freedom Index, and on the Impunity Index created by the Committee to Protect Journalists--somewhere in the vicinity of Iraq and Somalia. Even under the regime of the assassinated Benigno Aquino, Jr's son, Benigno Aquino III, over 30 journalists were killed, according to the National Union of Jour-nalists of the Philippines. A bottleneck in the judicial system and a culture of impunity means there is little justice for victims and their families.

At a forum to mark World Press Freedom Day in April 2015, both US Ambassador to the Philippines Philip S. Goldberg and United Nations Resident Coordinator Terence Jones brought up the extra-judicial killings of journalists in the Philippines as barri-ers to press freedom. While the number of killings has declined in recent years, Ambassador Goldberg said, "We all have to work so that number becomes zero." In his speech, Jones added: "Quality journalism enables citizens to make informed decisions about their society's development. It also works to expose injustice, corruption and the abuse of power." But the power of the press to improve society is weakened when people are afraid for their lives.

Tito Freddie had not been killed for his writing; he'd passed away at age 40 after a series of debilitating medical problems. But that left much of his life's work undone. My sister Liza messaged me the image of a 1984 letter Tito Freddie had sent. I showed it to Alice, Freddie's widow, as we sat together at her dark apartment.

She cried as she read it. In the letter he described a project he wanted to start, a biography of our common ancestor, Captain Pedro Navarro--only one of many projects that he did not have time to complete before his death.

"He wrote beautifully, didn't he?" she said. She herself would die only a few months after I finally met her. As I shared a meal with Alice and their daughter, Lyrah--herself an award-winning writer who currently teaches at the University of the Philippines Diliman--they talked about the hard times the family faced after Tito Freddie's death. There were medical bills to pay and children to get through school. They moved residences many times and along the way, Alice sold Freddie's book collection, over 7000 pieces, as many as the Philippines had islands, to help pay the bills.

The only people I met in the States who knew Freddie's work had studied Filipino literature, while almost everyone I asked in Manila was not only familiar with his work, but had known him personally. His roots in the literary community were deep. He founded the Philippine Literary Arts Council (PLAC) along with Gémino H. Abad, Cirilo F. Bautista, Ricardo M. de Ungria, and Alfred A. Yuson. In searching for Tito Freddie, I reached out to his friends, talking to Yuson, Bautista, and others. I found out that Tito Freddie acted in a film, Tikoy Aguiluz's *Boatman* (1984). He played a pimp.

Back in 1989, when my grandmother had broken the news that my pen pal had died, she had handed me Turtle Voices in Uncertain Weather, Tito Freddie's posthumous collection. I carried that book with me to college, my first apartments, graduate school, back and forth across the country and all the way back to Manila. Wherever I had a home, Turtle Voices was beside me the way that Gideon's Bible reliably sits in every hotel bedside's drawer. I especially loved the poem, "They Don't Think Much about Us in America," and returned to it often, when the micro-aggressions of daily life as an

Asian American got me down. I related to the anger in these lines:

> The only problem is
> they don't think much
> about us
> in America.
> That's where Manila's
> just as small as Guam is.

There are also playful poems where the stanzas formed shapes on the page. Those poems made me feel braver about experimenting with the page.

Tito Freddie's final poems traveled with me throughout my life along with, as I later realized, a note of introduction from his friend, Isagani Cruz. The same Isagani Cruz who--long before I'd put together the connection--mentored me and made possible my return to the Philippines. Even though Tito Freddie was long gone, I felt he was still guiding me, leading me to people and experiences that would help me progress as a writer. If I could not have my promised visit with Tito Freddie, his many friends was a good proxy.

A few days later, I knelt at Freddie's grave and ran my finger across the stone inscription: *The carpenter no longer sings*. The epitaph came from Tito Freddie's poem from *In Memoriam*, written after Aquino's assassination. Although this was my first visit to his grave, I had walked past it many times to visit my grandparents and godparents a few rows away. Tito Freddie was buried steps away from the same grandmother who would hand deliver his letters and books to me in Boston. I had traveled halfway around the world to search for my uncle in the Philippines, but his words have always been beside me. When I thought about my topics as a writer: undocumented immigrants in the US, my decision to remove my breasts and ovaries in order to prevent cancer, and other challenges, I felt Tito Freddie's courage had inspired me.

When I reread the letter that Tito Freddie wrote to my twelve-year old self, I realized that I had misread his line. He was prolific, but also careful and thoughtful with his words. He wrote, "So I hope you do grow up to be a good writer." What did he mean by "a good writer?" Good as in skilled or talented? Or good as in performing good deeds? Whichever way you meant it, Tito Freddie, I hope so, too.

An Odyssey

by Kazim Ali

Day like rain, a cast iron crow
Furling its wings in thin emptiness
My heavy body holds the wound
Deep inside black iron cloud

Raining down when the body fails
Wild thick it spring
No lesson in compassion
No cold hand season

Sun unreckon I dissolve
To summer hanging I bring
Dispersal of seeds legion
Mentor in the epic

With fake face and wisdom
Storm invest a second reason
Somehow calm of the ungrey crowd
Somehow still their war hungry violins

the long road to self-love

by Kat Geddes

my Korean mother eats nattō for breakfast.
I used to watch her swallow
strings of soybeans with a mixture of curiosity and
quiet revulsion.
every time I opened the fridge
a waft of nattō would hit me in the face
and I'd run away
from her
from nattō
from my Otherness.

these days, my mother won't return my calls
and I don't know where my sister is.
she didn't leave a note
or say goodbye.
so I find my Otherness
in Asian grocery stores,
steaming ramen bowls,
pickled radish rolls,
and somewhere in Aisle 10
between soy sauce and chilli oil,
my four-eyed, fourteen year old self
stares back at me
reproachfully.

somewhere on the road
from awkward adolescence,
I left this girl behind.
I built fortresses of grades and resumes
degrees and accolades
until my paper self was just as white as my
surname would suggest.
because Otherness was rudderless
and I was constantly adrift,
haunting
the empty space
between
two boxes on a form.

I craved the certainty of categories
to keep self-worth
from leaking
from the seams.
because belonging
seemed to matter more than blood,
and anyway what good was east meets west
when all it brought was bitterness,
a broken home,
a shattered phone,
two parents who were really poles
spreading
further
and further
apart.

perhaps a paler version of myself
could forget the broken glass.

so blending in became the thing
I'd struggle to perfect,
with English words in dialects
as local as the native trees
whose sunburnt arms trailed
jacaranda leaves in spring.

I treasured every freckle earnt
in hours in the sun
as evidence of dissemblance
from my mother's spotless skin.
my freckles were constellations of conformity
with magazines and TV screens and
friends I desperately craved.
I'd have no roots, no past, no pain
just silent shame at the broken words
that tumbled from my mother's lips,
at the smell of nattō
in our fridge.

the weird thing is
these days
I seem to crave it even more.
I stock my shelves with miso paste, tofu slabs, galbi
beef, as if the motion of my teeth
could somehow bring me closer to
my mother tongue,
repent for my rejection
of her Otherness
and mine,
reclaim my place
on dusty shelves
in the corners of the frames.

these days
I fill the silence of unanswered calls
with the crackle and hiss of frying fish,
sizzling beef, crackling pork,
all the things she used to make.
maybe the taste
could dull the ache
of all the ways
I disappointed her.

these days
I watch friends ferment kimchi
with a sense of deep offense,
why wasn't I consulted?
don't they know I'm half-Korean?
I never thought I'd wear
my Otherness like a badge
when it used to be a
bruise
appearing slowly
like polaroids
in unexpected places.

isn't it strange
to develop a thirst for pigment
just as the world is starting to spit you out.
as white supremacists march the streets,
troll the web, occupy the Office,
as borders close their ears to
screaming babes,
cries muffled
by the sea's embrace.

only the ocean
opened its arms.

isn't it strange
to start to love
the alien above the sink
whose brows you've furrowed every day
searching for a way to bear
the puzzle of her nose, his eyes, her hair.
because there
on your face
they're still together.

isn't it strange
to start to love yourself
just as the continental shelf begins to crack
to split apart
beneath your feet
with every xenophobic tweet.
just as the Cheeto in Chief
raises an army of undead,
minds numbed by myths
hearts frozen by hatred,
wounds soothed by
white privilege.
an army of White Walkers
tumbling
from his vending machine
of lies, collecting
hate crimes
like old coins.

these days
I wear my DNA like diamonds.
each strand sings the song of
immigrants
souls who scaled walls
of brick and bone
whispered strange words on
thirsty tongues to open
secret passageways
to safety.
parents who taught me how to grow,
placed me in the window of opportunity
so I could feel the sun on my skin and
know
that only the sky was the limit.

after all, when we return to dust
what will we have but the traces of places
where those who loved us
hugged us
and made us feel whole.
human.

so let the Cheeto in Chief
trade in Wall St for war crimes,
let his beauty pageant of bigots
compete for his reflection,
because we will
never disappear.

just as the ocean returns to hug the shore
every time it's sent away,
we'll gather under every milky newborn moon
to plot and plan and prune
the briars of intolerance,
the bloody walls of ignorance,
we'll march in every street and town
and stain your eardrums with the sound of
certainty in dignity
of
every
human
life.

this is a call to arms
for every bad hombre, every nasty woman,
every muslim, every mexican, every person who
believes that we hold these truths to be
self evident.
because southern trees once bore strange fruit
because we said
hands up don't shoot
because we are
the resistance.

and it's
our future
to claim.

You Had Me at Beheading!

by Steve Almond

*F*or a mid-list author not currently under indictment, I receive lots of hate mail. Back when I publicly resigned as an Adjunct Professor of Bitterness at Boston College to protest the selection of then-Secretary of State Condoleezza Rice as commencement speaker, for instance, my email box filled with hundreds of notes from patriotic citizens. They threatened to sic Navy Seals on me. They compared me to Hitler and Stalin. They said my daughter looked like a maggot. It was grand.

So when I wrote my new book "Against Football"—which probes the variegated corruptions of America's most popular and profitable sport—I was braced for some extreme reactions. America being what America is these days, I was not disappointed.

I'd like to share a few of these letters, along with responses to my loyal correspondents. (Note: the letters themselves are recorded here verbatim, though I've used pseudonyms.)

Ready? Hut hut yikes!

Dear Steve,

There is something immoral in everything: gay sex, gambling, tattoos, writing books to make money. Watching football isn't immoral. Grown men get paid millions of dollars to put there [sic] brains on the line. It's there [sic] choice to do so. High School and College not as many injuries. There's a reason football is the greatest, most popular game on the planet. People like violence, they like physical aggression, it's as old as the Roman Coloseum [sic].

Signed,

Barry Kutner

*

Dear Barry,

You cover a lot of ground here, so let's take these one a time.

First, your list of immoral activities is awesome. It's like the Ten Commandments as conceived by Gomer Pyle.

Second, the reason NFL players get paid so much money is because fans like us are addicted to football. I know this sounds confusing, because we're used to the media scapegoating players and league officials and owners, and thus insulating us from our role as sponsors. The moral question is: should we underwrite the game?

Third, yes, high school and college players do not suffer as high a percentage of injuries as pros. This is because they are not as big and strong and fast as the pros, and also because injuries to the human body—in particular the brain—are incremental.

Fourth, people do like violence and aggression. They also like heroin and deep-fried Twinkies and porn. Despite the ardent enabling of capitalism, taking pleasure in an experience isn't actually a moral justification for having that experience. It's just proof that you have a functioning limbic system, like the rest of the animal kingdom. What sets human beings apart from other animals is that we come equipped with a conscience. We are capable of imagining the suffering of others. Without this capacity, life would be a Hieronymus Bosch painting.

Finally, historians generally view the Colosseum as a symptom of the imperial decadence that eventually doomed the Roman Empire. I'm not sure you want to be citing that particular piece of architecture to bolster your argument for football's enduring supremacy.

*

Dear Steve,
You are the Biggest Faggot.
Signed,
Bill Ives

Dear Bill,
Thank you for your thoughtful letter. I have to admit that it came at the right moment. For years I've been working hard to prove just how big a faggot I could become. I developed a lisp and a swishy gait and grew out a mustache and started wearing tight denim.

At first, this desire to display my hyper-homosexuality was just a personal thing. But eventually, like all truly ambitious faggots, I started following the Top Queen Rankings (TQR) posted on the Secret Gay Internet That We're Not Supposed to Tell Straight People About. And pretty soon I didn't just want to follow the action. I wanted to *compete*. I doubled my workout and moisturizing regimen. I memorized the lyrics to *every* Stephen Sondheim musical ever written. I manscaped compulsively and started dressing in hot pink leiderhosen and LCD displays. And obviously I had lots and lots of gay sex in public settings.

If other faggots were administering oral sex to ten strangers in a softly lit bathhouse, well then, I would suck off a dozen strapping lumberjacks in a crowded public square, and make sure my efforts were streaming live on-line. I had so much anal sex last summer that the training staff put my rectum on injured reserved for, like, five weeks.

But that's just the way I am. When it comes to the TQRs, Will, I show up ready to gay every day. I give 110 percent, regardless of the risks. I leave it all on the field. I guess what I'm trying to say is that your support means a lot to me.

Steve

*

Dear Steve,

You're living proof that if you scratch a liberal you'll find a fascist. We read your book and found it to be a perfect example of how leftists operate. If people organize a book burning, you're up in arms. But when it comes to destroying a whole way of life—and yes, football is a way of life for many of us—you have no compunction. The good news is that your self-righteous bleating will never move the needle one bit. We consider your call for a boycott to be a ringing endorsement. Pass the nachos, dude.

Signed,

Anna and Cam

Anna and Cam,

Many things confuse me and your letter is one of them. As I understand it, I am both destroying your way of life and, at the same time, completely powerless to destroy your way of life. I feel I should tell you that this is how I feel as the parent of three young children every single minute of every day.

Steve

*

Dear Steve,

The next reporter that ISIS wants to behead, I hope we can give them you in his or her stead.

Signed,

Lex

Dear Lex,

Totally get what you're after here but I'm concerned about the logistics. ISIS is a fundamentalist movement among Sunni extremists. We don't really "give" them journalists to behead. It's more a situation where they *capture* journalists then behead them for publicity purposes. ISIS doesn't appear to negotiate with Westerners. So it's going to be tough to arrange the sort of swap you're endorsing.

But I'm willing to trust that you've got a connection to someone high up in the ISIS hierarchy, or can establish one, because you seem like an intelligent, resourceful person. But you've still got the dilemma of convincing ISIS that I, Steve Almond, am worth beheading. This could get tricky, because I'm not a foreign correspondent or even really a journalist. I'm just a football fan who wrote a book about his tortured decision to turn away from the game. In this sense, I'm actually kind of anti-American, if you think about it. Which makes me kind of pro-ISIS. I actually publicly opposed the war in Iraq.

But who knows? Maybe I've done the math wrong here. ISIS does seem to recognize the American proclivity for bloodlust, the way in which we can't quite turn away from violent spectacles. I also do a lot of whining in "Against Football" about how the NFL peddles a medieval worldview when it comes to defining gender and denigrating women and gays. In theory, then, ISIS members might be huge NFL fans.

Likewise, they might be utterly smitten by a guy like you, Lex. After all, when someone writes a book you disagree with your first impulse is to have his head chopped off in public. That's straight out of the ISIS playbook, brother.

Steve

*

Steve,

When you stop eating meat from factory farming, stop idolizing the military, stop wearing clothes made in third world countries, and stop supporting the putrid garbage that wastes society's resources from TV and Hollywood (and the excessive money paid to entertainers as a start), I'll stop watching football.

Okay?

Caspar

Dear Caspar,

Can I tell you a secret? Sometimes, late at night, when we know we should be doing something noble such as reading a book or prepping tofu for tomorrow's vegan potluck, me and the wife watch us some dumbass television. I'm talking rock-bottom scuzzfest shit. *Rock of Love. Sister Wives.* Like that.

And yet, in the morning, we continue to make what we consider to be ethical decisions. We don't eat meat. We compost and recycle compulsively. We take public transportation. We donate to Doctors Without Borders. This is how life works for those of us living in the absurd abundance of America. We are all complicit in our own ways.

But it sounds to me like you're using this argument more strategically. You really love watching football. And your excuse for doing so—knowing that it's a profoundly violent game run by greedy billionaires, etc.—is that moral perfection itself is impossible.

This is a pretty failsafe rationale, but it puts you in some unsavory company. I'm thinking, specifically, of The Misfit from the famous Flannery O'Connor short story "A Good Man Is Hard to Find." Here's how he viewed things:

> Jesus was the only One that ever raised the dead and He shouldn't have done it. He shown everything off balance. If He did what He said, then it's nothing for you to do but throw away everything and follow Him, and if He didn't, then it's nothing for you to do but enjoy the few minutes you got left

the best way you can by killing somebody or burning down his house or doing some other meanness to him. No pleasure but meanness.

Your letter implies that living in a fallen world grants you the right to sin as you please. That doesn't make you a righteous man, Caspar. It makes you a religious psychopath.
Steve

*

Steve,
I read your book. Here's the problem with all your claims about sexism: men and women aren't equal. Man is physically stronger than woman.
Signed,
South Shore Glen

Glen,
Have you ever pushed a small human being out of your body? No?
Then shut your fucking mouth.
Steve

*

Hey First Cut,
Having read your book, I am wondering if you were just not skilled enough to play in high school and now want to take your aggression out on the best sport in the world because you were denied?
Sam Kitchell

Sam,
Probably. I think most football fans, if they're honest, are driven in part by slavish envy. We all wish we'd been bigger and stron-

ger and faster and we weren't and that's why we're on some sofa hoping that our team beats your team, so we can feel at least a vicarious sense of dominion. It's pretty pathetic when you look at it straight on.

I should mention that I was (and am) insanely competitive. Part of the reason I quit playing sports in college *was* that I realized I wasn't ever going to be great. I didn't have the skill or commitment. But it's also true that I found the world of jocks kind of dull. They didn't have much to say. Being good at a sport was all that mattered. The mindset was conformist. It felt like a pretty small life.

To some extent, being a fan has that same comforting smallness. You know where you stand because the standings tell you.

I guess for me leaving football was about trying to live a larger, more doubtful life. That's what I tell myself anyway. What do you tell yourself?

Steve

*

Steve,

Read your book. (What I could get through.) Why don't you simply admit the truth and write, "I used to love football until my team [the Oakland Raiders] started to suck." Go Seahawks!!!

Danielle

Dear Danielle,

I admit it: I used to love football until my team started to suck. What's more: if the Raiders had been great over the past few years, I doubt I would have written "Against Football." I would have been preoccupied with the annihilating ecstasy of feeling like a winner, just like you and the rest of the Seahawk fans I met recently in Seattle.

Maybe this is America, Doris. Maybe this is what it means to be an American in this age of private terrors. Maybe we need a beautiful savage game to make us feel alive and united. That's how I felt when the Raiders were winning, when Kenny Stabler was throwing up his wounded ducks for Cliff Branch to snag and Rich Gannon was scrambling for impossible first downs. I'm sure that's how you feel right now. I envy you that.

But remember that winning never lasts. It's a bad deal you make with fate. Soon enough your Seahawks will suck. They'll be Brian Bosworth and Jim Zorn, not Russell Wilson and Richard Sherman. Not saying that to be a jerk. It's just the truth. What will you do then, Doris? Is there some chance that you'll regard my book any differently? That you'll see it as a lamentation for the childish needs we carry into adulthood? Or the manner in which those needs are ruthlessly exploited for profit?

Consider this: at the end of our own fourth quarters, how will we look back upon our decisions in this life? Will we cling to the conviction that it was wise to give so much of our hearts and minds and wallets to a game? Or will we feel such attentions might have been better spent on our own struggles—to love and create and forgive? Will we think back to the grace and heroism we found in those bright stadiums? And will that be enough to cancel out our regrets?

Steve

After the President Calls Citizens "Sons of Bitches"

by Anne Champion

As I watch the line of men drop to their knees, refusing to praise
the God of country, the most jealous and vengeful God of all,
I am thinking of the bitches. The bitches that poured love

into their sons' bodies, that took in pain like the mournful note
of an expanding accordion, the bitches who trace the half moons
of their C-section scars whenever they see another son slaugh-
    tered,

whose lovers kiss their stretch marks and their deflated breasts
    that nursed
life into their lives. I imagine those bitches peeled the potatoes,
    hummed
Bible hymns, bought football jerseys, wore the school's colors and
    danced

in the bleachers at home games, cheering, *That's my baby!*
with such a pride that their sons started to think their bodies mat-
    tered.
Maybe those bitches warned them, or maybe they didn't have to,

that the beer guzzling crowd will adore everything their bodies
can do for them, will roar when they sprint across the field
like meteor showers, will collapse into ecstasy with every touch-
    down,

but they will not love a body that doesn't bow to compliance.
I wonder what the bitches think when they see their boys
on their knees, their moment of prayer that demands that anthems

be held accountable to their promises. My mother would not be
    called a bitch
because of the lessons she taught me: that the people in the Mid-
    dle East
were brainwashed to think their country is chosen by their god,

that people that lived in communism were too afraid to overthrow
their governments or even speak ill of them, that we were the only
    country
in the world that was truly free and righteous. We lie to our chil-
    dren

so that we can lie to ourselves comfortably as adults. America's
greatest triumph: we will worship the flag even when the flag
becomes a shroud. I'm sure the bitches know this. The men on
    their knees

certainly do, as the president that we haven't even attempted to
    overthrow
says that their jobs should be taken from them, calls their mothers
bitches, assures there are good people marching for white su-
    premacy,

and promises to break the will of their bodies through law and
    order.
And we watch, knees locked and hands on our hearts, as bullets
    tear
through the bodies of these sons of these bitches,

as they are on their knees with their hands in the air,
as the bitches drop to their knees in front of their coffins,
and as the sons refuse to perform allegiance to our apathy,

silently taking the knee and bowing their heads, while the lens of
    history
flashes to capture another moment of our collective shame
and the bitches bear witness to the quiet defiance their love bore.

Our Cultural Amnesia About Sexual Assault

by Alexandria Marzano-Lesnevich

*D*ating women made me realize how much sexual violence we were all trying to ignore.

The first night I kissed a woman was clear and cold. The wind smelled of snow, and as we walked the paths of Boston's Public Garden, the streetlights making the frost around us sparkle, we kept our hands shoved deep in our coat pockets. Her coat was a brilliant emerald green that seemed to glow in the light. It matched the color of her eyes.

That coat was the first thing I'd ever noticed about her, a week before. We'd met online but had traded no pictures. I'd done plenty of online dating but never before with another woman. She was much more experienced but knew enough to be careful with my shyness. Finally, we'd agreed to meet in a coffee shop. Leaving the train station to walk the few blocks there, I'd spotted a woman in that beautiful green coat, golden hair tumbling in waves over her shoulders. I'd never seen her before — and yet. Somehow I thought it was her. I walked to the coffee shop half-hoping, half-knowing it was her. And half-wishing it wasn't. That my life wasn't about to change.

But then the coffee shop door opened. And the woman in the green coat walked in.

Then, a week of coffees and drinks. Each time we'd met, I'd gotten nervous and rambled to her like a friend — then pretty much turned and ran as soon as the date, or whatever it was, was over. I hadn't touched her. She hadn't touched me. Just: ramble. Run. The night before, we'd finally had dinner together at a hippie-ish Tibetan place where nothing cost more than a few dollars and the wooden tables were beat up. When she sat down at the table, she'd slid her coat off her shoulders and revealed that she was wearing a silver sequin top slit down deep between her breasts. I stopped drinking my tea. I'm pretty sure I gulped. She grinned, and I got the point: we weren't just friends. Could I please get over my nerves, already? But at the end of the night, I ran again.

Now we stood atop a little stone arched bridge in the garden. It could have belonged in a fairy tale. Might have had a billy goat beneath it. She took her hands out of her pockets and rubbed them together, then turned and faced me. Close enough that I could see how the wind had made her eyes water, her eyelashes glisten. We were going to kiss — I could feel that we were going to kiss — and though the wind rushed cold around me, time stretched.

She looked up at me. Those eyes. Then she said, "There's something about me you should know."

And she told me her father had sexually assaulted her. For years.

There was a time — right after the day the *Access Hollywood* tape came out in 2016 — when it seemed like we might finally be ready to pay serious attention to the prevalence of sexual assault in this country. When it seemed like ignoring it might actually, for once, hurt someone other than those of us who live with it in our bodies.

Typing that now, though, seems almost naïve, with President Trump in the Oval Office and Clarence Thomas still sitting comfortably on the Supreme Court.

I listened to her talk. We didn't kiss then. Mostly, I was quiet, watching her. I asked some gentle questions when it seemed like she wanted them. Afterward, we walked around the park for a long time. Eventually we did kiss, and I remember the surprise of how sweet her mouth tasted and how full her lips were — but mostly I remember her words. My quiet.

And my shock.

Because while she spoke I realized that I'd never considered this part of dating women. That dating women — statistically radically more likely to be sexually assaulted than men — would mean navigating the memories they carried in their bodies. And navigating how to carry mine.

Was I supposed to tell her then that I, too, had been abused by a family member — in my case my grandfather?

For the ten years I'd spent in the closet, I'd worried about so many things that might happen if I came out. I'd worried about my loved ones' reactions. I'd worried about how I'd make a family, if I couldn't have what I'd grown up with: parents who were married, children who were biologically from both parents. Gay marriage was such an obscure idea, that when I'd told my college-thesis adviser I wanted to look at the legal theories in support of it in 2001, he'd waved off the idea. We were in New York City. He was a deeply liberal sociologist. But gay marriage? That was so fringe it sounded crazy.

So I worried about how I'd be perceived. I worried whether being out as gay would harm the legal career I had then planned.

(It must, I thought. How could it not?) I even worried that if people knew I'd been abused, they would think that that was why I was gay. Like that had turned me gay. That seemed like the most horrible idea of all. That even if I grew comfortable with my desire for women, others would dismiss it as just a side effect caused by a man's abuse. There are times, when I look back now at this list, that I'm dumbstruck by it. How afraid I was to just be who I am. What did I really think would be so bad? Yet how quickly social change would come was unthinkable then. So I worried.

But with all I worried about, I had never once worried about how I'd handle someone else's sexual trauma. I had male friends — two I knew about — who'd been abused, but I'd never dated them. I'd never thought about why I'd avoided it — but on some level, I'd known why. The idea had seemed hopelessly complicated: Who would hold whom, if a flashback came? What if both of us had a flashback at the same time? How could that possibly feel safe?

But then I started dating women. And soon, it was impossible to avoid.

The Trump administration doesn't lack for scandals and should-be scandals. Right now the internet is awash in tales of Harvey Weinstein's monstrous behavior. We're in a moment where the topic has risen sharply, and change seems possible. But I worry it will die away again in the endless ebb of our news cycle. Remember Jerry Sandusky? Nate Parker? Woody Allen? Roman Polanski? Casey Affleck? Bill Cosby?

The conversation flared and then died then, too.

Yet there are many of us — far too many of us — for whom it never really dies down. Memories live in our bodies and in our communities. When I began teaching creative writing, every term, a third of my students would self-disclose as having been abused or assaulted. (Though once, when I observed this to a class, a student approached me afterward, her face grim. "You know one-third's just those of us who've told you," she said.) The CDC estimates that nearly one in five women have been raped. Forty percent of black women have been subject to "coercive sexual conduct" by age eighteen. And surveys of sexual minority populations — LGBTQ people, like me — consistently show that 30 to 40 percent report having been sexually abused.

Each time I read a number like this, I recoil. I want to push back. I want to push back because I don't want it to be true. And I want to push back because there's still part of me that feels so alone in this experience — even knowing the percentage. That felt so alone each time I discovered a new lover had this in her past, too, and felt just as alone as I did.

That's the irony: Most of us do feel alone in it. A culture that's always moving on to the next thing, always stranding us with our experience, makes sure we do.

The woman in the green coat and I dated for months. She was my first girlfriend — but not my last. I think back over the years of dating women that have followed, and I arrive at the statistic above: yes, 40 percent.

On generous days, I want to think that some of the silence isn't malicious. That maybe the reason the culture stops talking about it so quickly is that a lot of people can afford to. That maybe it's just natural they stop thinking about it, if they don't have memories that live in their body, that make their breath run cold with panic when a moment that should be pleasure becomes a memory of terror. Or if they don't live in communities in which assault is rampant, and have to see their lover gasp with memory. They can fool themselves into thinking it's another person's problem. Just some poor person's trauma.

But then I remember the statistics. And I think of the #metoo hashtag. No matter how alone I feel sometimes, it's not just some communities. It's all of us.

So on my most generous days? On those days, I allow myself to hope that maybe yes, this is finally the moment. Maybe the culture is actually ready to hear us. Maybe it will catch up to what many of us have been living for years. And finally—finally—change.

Ode to Slug Disguised as Letter to a Men's Rights Activist

by Kendra DeColo

I imagine we both like burritos
and enjoy sitting for long stretches
at a desk half-heartedly searching

through the forested backlogs
of Porn Hub to relish the chafe
and exhale of deliverance. Or how

I sometimes get aroused
via humiliation. Or shame.
Or the very thought

that I am a sexual being
and my desire is folded
up inside of me like a wet

envelope. But I hope that's where
we part ways, as the slug
parts from its semen-like

trail, and shall we consider,
for a moment, the slug, whose inscription
of swampy air and brittle

light purchases a particular
parcel of disgust in my chest;
little cavity of unnameable

ooze pilfered with a thwack
on hot summer days—
the only living thing I felt entitled

to hurt—not kill—as a child
(although I'd stomp
whole amphitheaters of ants

in the heat-sueded dirt.) Yes I wanted
to hurt them, for the very fact
I thought they couldn't feel—

their surplus of congealed
dew, alien-like snot. Jesus cum.
Yes. That coveted and bloated

with mystery. I wanted to know
what engine gurgled inside
like a melted gear, the sun's hooked

cock. To find the seam in their seamless
body. Maybe that's what it's like
to feel so entitled to something

as when I look at the moon-
soaked sky, pearled and
apostrophied with clouds

and know that my heart
and lungs will eventually unravel
like cashmere in a moth's spangled maw

and in that moment I feel something
like a rage and lust for the world,
receding just when I want it most.

Q County Colored Penitentiary

by Sonya Larson

Decades earlier, Kensington was not "Kensington." He was simply Abe. And he probably would have turned out like every other white boy in the county if he hadn't, that day in June, gone deep into the forest and come upon a secret prison.

He was twelve: fine-haired, skinny-armed, and patterned with blue bruises from rumbling up every staircase in the estate. The nanny tried to grab his ankles, make him sit, here, eat your supper, the dinner bell still clanging on its hook, but Abe enjoyed wriggling from clenched fingernails and suddenly bursting free. He'd bound out the west veranda like a dog, napkin flying at his neck, to the buzzing creek as the sun sunk under Quitman.

Boys of twelve were warned against hiking in that forest, but as he set out with his father's walking stick, he saw that grown-ups were ridiculous. It was just a swamp with vines, putrid water, slicked branches arching from mud. He understood that Kensington Forest was his great-great-great-great-granddaddy Henry Abramaside Kensington, settled by way of the Mayflower itself, but this fact meant little to Abe then. By lunchtime (he noticed, because he'd forgotten to pack a lunch) he was miles deeper than he'd ever been, beyond the skimpiest shoreline of trees, beyond the would-be shouts of the nanny. His foot got sucked into a burping sink-hole, but that was all. And the "outdoorsmen vestments" he'd been gifted at Christmas—sheepskin boots and a leather-hooded wind cape? Heavy, cumbersome, and useless useless useless.

He did feel foolish about the food. His stomach gnawed and the forest grew loud with croaking frogs, squawking birds, and the leaves frothing overhead. Abe plodded forward—perhaps the feel-ing would pass—until his knees trembled and his vision watered. Where were the berries in this stupid forest? In the distance strange screeches echoed through the trees, like a train braking on its iron girders. He was delirious.

But was that not the sound of screeching metal? It was. It had to be. Abe wandered toward it, to where the sunlight slid more readily through the canopy. There was a clearing and a long gray building that resembled a horse stable. Surrounding all was a tall wire fence, the gate of which was being heaved open by two figures with long, black braids.

Who could say why Abe hid behind a tree? Some instinct that knew the trouble of quiet. The two were foreigners—coolies. They wore wrinkled robes to their ankles, with rifles slung diagonally across their backs. A faint beard on one, the other clean-shaven. They turned to each other to trade a ring of keys, and by the curves of their cheekbones Abe saw that they were not two men but one man and one woman. A real Chinawoman, with a belt full of tools! They resembled the China folk who managed his father's commis-saries, but Abe did not recognize their faces. Silently they worked, entering the fence and locking the door behind them. With a sud-den clink the woman dropped her keys; the man stooped to the grass and returned them to her palm. She grinned at him. He quick-kissed her cheek.

The horse stable was unlike those at home, with no windows or obvious slits for ventilation. Just a long rectangle of steel bolted to vertical beams, like a boxcar abandoned on the dirt. The surrounding yard had been cleared of branches overhead, the Mississippi sun flashing off the metal roof. It must have been baking in there. Nearby was a crate of feed, a pump handle for a well, and two buckets.

The woman worked the pump and the man eased the wooden lid off of the crate. Drunken flies floated up and he shooed them away. He scooped a bucket of feed—dry corn, by the sound of it—and carried it to the horse stable. The long wall did not extend fully to the ground; a six-inch trough had been dug along the length of it. The coolie poured out the feed, walking backwards. The tongues of the horses licked it up, the line of yellow disappearing.

Then the Chinawoman did a curious thing. She walked to the horse stable and knocked three times. From under the wall appeared a shallow tray, as if by magic. What kind of horse could do that? The woman kneeled and lifted it with the edges of her fingertips, her mouth twisted, looking and not looking at the same time. She hurried the basin to a boulder and tipped the contents onto the rock. It did not smell like normal manure.

That was when Abe knew: those were no horses.

The coolies washed their hands and left along a path behind the building—to the other side of the woods, to where Abe had wanted to venture all along. But all that now seemed unimportant. This place, whatever it was, seemed to be the end of the woods itself.

He needed food. He'd have to be quick. He climbed the fence, darted to the crate and lifted the lid, but inside the walls were coated in a furry blue mold. He turned to the yellow line of corn disappearing under the wall. His stomach rumbled. He crouched up to the metal, its bottom edge cut so that it frayed with jagged teeth. A single, expert finger emerged, lowering to pick up each kernel one by one.

It was a Negro's finger. Further down the wall, another one. And a third. Would they hear the jerking of his heart? Abe spied a smattering of kernels in the powdery dirt. He held his breath. He kneeled. He swept them up and into his pocket.

The finger stopped. It seemed to be listening. "Who there?" A man's deep voice echoed from inside the box. "Who's it out there?" Years later Abrams would remember that it was a not a shrill voice, not wild or deranged. Instead it was a searching voice, listening through the dark.

"It a deer?" came someone else, whispering and tense.

The first voice spoke again. "Who there?"

What Abe would not remember was how he scrambled back over that fence to the safety of the woods or how he found the rock to catch his breath. He would only remember shaking the kernels into his sweat-glistened hand. It was so similar to the corn his father approved weekly on the groundskeeper's bill, the corn that traveled from wagon to commissary to burlap to barrel to scoop, so the Negro croppers of Kensington acreage could feed the mules and reap the cotton. Abe slurped one into his mouth. It didn't feel like food at all—too hard and resistant and without taste. He bit. It wiggled down his throat like a swallowed tooth.

Who there? The voice knew that he was no deer.

The corn was enough. He made it back that day, and when the nanny came running out of the veranda, weeping onto the un-mowed grass, hugging him angrily, demanding to know *where? why? do you hear me?* His mother and even his father emerged, fidgeting in the doorway. But Abe could not speak. Or rather, words themselves seemed hollow, so useless to describe the how and what and why of where he'd been.

They bathed him, fed him, reclothed him. The nanny would

not let him out of her sight. The steaming bathtub, the bowls of soup, the headboard sandbagged with pillows. She left him only once, to fetch more tea, her swishing slippers hurrying up the stairs.

She sat on the bed, sinking the mattress near his knees. She pulled a brush hard against his scalp. "Has my mother gone to bed?" he asked.

"Blessedly, yes." She shook her head. "Such a long day they done had."

"Maggie," he said, "did you know that there's a building in the woods out there? It's long, it looks like a horse barn. But it isn't a horse barn. There are people inside. I saw them myself, I swear."

Ms. Margaret was quiet. She was brushing his hair in steady strokes, not looking at his eyes but at the space above them. "Strange," she said slowly. "What a day indeed."

"And the people in there—they're Negroes, I think." He paused and corrected himself; Maggie didn't like to be called that. "Coloreds, I mean. And there were these coolies who gave them food and water in a bucket."

Ms. Margaret pulled back the brush and ripped the tangled hairs from the bristles. "Must be on old Plawson's property. Up there's all kinds of crazy."

His mother had a similar response. "I can't imagine what that Plawson has in mind these days." She wiped her nose with her scalloped handkerchief and squeezed Abe's shoulder. "Just please don't bother your father about it—the sorghum prices are eating him alive."

The next morning seemed to last all day. Objects looked sharper and yet more mysterious. His curtains quivered with puffballs like a fishnet pulled dripping from the sea. Outside, a single geyser of a tree shot from the grass into a thousand sprays of needles. Even his tea tasted different, harsh and scraping over the beads of his tongue.

His father, who Abe dutifully avoided, now seemed to avoid Abe. He stood up when Abe entered the parlor, remembering a phone call to be made or an errand needing immediate attention. More and more he appeared to Abe in hallways, in the entrances and exits of rooms, before the hurrying-on of coats, the flaring of umbrellas. He smelled the lingering trail of his pipe tobacco, pungent as overripe flowers.

Every day was like this except Thursday, when the County Commissioner, Warren Panette, and a rotation of associates came for bridge-playing in the West Parlor. Abe would help Maggie deliver glasses of bourbon just so he could breathe in the shuffling of cards, the generous laughter, the pipe smoke curling in the lamplight. A bowl of boiled peanuts—cropper food, they joked— littered the table with papery shells. They spoke of elections and corn subsidies and sending President Wilson to hell themselves. It was the only time of the week when his father seemed to relax, his elbows leaning on the table and his eyes grinning through that long, thick beard like General Longstreet himself. He'd lift a glass from Abe's waiting tray and sip, nodding his eyes politely over the rim, as if Abe was not his son but a very appreciated young boy.

Abe grew up. Life carried on as planned: school in the schoolhouse, evening parties in the foyer, Saturday supper with the commissioner, and Sunday with the minister. But more and more, Abrams—as he started to call himself—was disgusted by it all. The gold-rimmed teacups, the sweaters shipped from his uncle vacationing in Brazil. "For your expeditions," read the note, as his relatives marveled at the softness of alpaca. Perhaps it was sent to make light of his rugged desires. He threw the sweater in his closet and slammed the door.

He hated it all. He read Whitman and Thoreau and avoided the budding girls his friends now idled around. He would escape to a particular tree, far from the yard, with hard bark and soft grass and the sun sinking until it hurt to read. *The setting sun is reflected from the windows of the almshouse,* he squinted. *As brightly as from the rich man's abode.* The beads, the braids, the debutante balls: he decided these things were new; they were a waste of time. But the river, the rocks, the wind rippling over the Delta: these things were old. On them he would depend.

He moved into the storeroom behind the stairs. He lived like a pauper, dragging only the quilt from his bed and a single box of candles. He would wash his underwear in a bucket, hanging their cold drippings to dry over chairbacks. Everyone agreed it was repulsive behavior, though his mother was initially amused. "There goes our little idealist," she'd smile as he trampled barefoot through the kitchen. "Good morning, Hawthorne." This continued until she found the wet sock plopped atop her heirloom cedar pie chest. His parents spent long evenings huddled by the East parlor fireplace, finally spending time together, united in trading theories and complaints.

He continued making soap and trimming his fingernails with a jackknife until, one day, he didn't want those either. That life, too, seemed phony, too full of showy effort. He moved back upstairs, albeit with sparser items than before: a single pillow, the same quilt, a mirror and a razor. Maggie emptied the washbucket on the grass, where it dried and faded.

It was not that he contemplated directly the lives of the men in the metal box. He did not. He imagined questions, yes, but he did not imagine their answers: how they managed to breathe, if there was any source of light, how they withstood the heat in summer and the frigidness in winter, how it smelled, what they spoke of, whether they knew if it was morning or evening, how they aimed into that shallow tray. He thought of these questions but not beyond them—such ideas were too remote to look at, like the other side of the moon.

One night he awoke to a hand gently shaking him. It was his mother, not Maggie. "Abe." Her voice warbled; she gulped air. "I'm so sorry, Abe." His father had died. A buggy accident while on business in Crenshaw. He tried to remember the last thing he said to his father. *See you at bridge?* But he could not remember.

In this way the Kensington land — all two hundred and thirty-six acres of it — became his. He employed his father's groundskeeper to manage it, went to college in Memphis, renounced God, cavorted with intellectuals, studied the emerging field of civil engineering, took a wife, and came home. His mother — just months before she, too, would pass — moved her things from the master bedroom into the remodeled guestroom, where Abrams had camped all those years before. He and his new wife folded up the old quilt and laid it at the foot of the bed. In the closet he discovered the old alpaca sweater — miraculously no moths had gotten to it. He pushed his head through the plush collar and walked to the full-length mirror. It fit.

At the window he inspected his land. In his absence the groundskeeper had done an admirable job — the early cotton was growing with vigor, and a new grid of irrigation ditches was working beautifully. Below, the cropper families had no doubt been planting since sunrise, dragging fertilizer sacks through the rows while their little ones sprinkled it from purses. And beyond them, the woods. Many times his father must have stood at this window, surveying what was his. Had he seen what Abrams saw? The same bent croppers and the dark backdrop of the forest? Did he see the past, or did he see the future?

Abrams did not know. But he would do things differently. He knew that.

They had one daughter.

They'd hoped for a gaggle of children romping through the

lilacs, but God would give them just the one. They named her Beatrice.

She was a drowsy child who yawned through her nose and enjoyed her bassinette more than any place else. Abrams and Mary took her to the fields themselves; they proudly released Ms. Margaret of her childcare duties, keeping her only for weekly cleanings and special events. It was Mary's idea—she was from St. Louis and a modern woman, her hair chin-cropped and her closet full of pants. She had studied chemistry, though she would obviously not be pursuing that in Quitman. Together they agreed on which rooms in the house were unnecessary and emptied the closets, stripped the beds, and shut the doors down the hallways. Mary loved camping and hiking and knew the names of plants, and Abrams adored her.

"Take that bonnet off of her," she said to Abrams, out in the grass. "Let her see the sun." They were having a picnic supper, right here, on his property: no suit jackets, no highback chairs, no heirloom pewter napkin rings, not even utensils. Just a sheet tossed over the grass and meaty sandwiches they ate by hand. Abrams removed the cotton eyelet bonnet from his baby's head. She blinked, rubbed her face, and sneezed repeatedly.

"Oh dear," said Mary, fitting the bonnet back on.

"Maybe you'd prefer a big, yellow, fragrant daisy?" said Abrams, leaning one into Bee's nose. She batted it away. "No daisies," he said. "Noted." Then she squirmed and squeaked until they gathered the half-eaten sandwiches and the glasses of wine, and he slung the sheet over one shoulder and hurried the whole affair inside.

He bought books on the subject of rocks and their categorization, collecting specimens from his property and lining them up atop her bureau: shale, clay, slate, granite. He would teach Bee the ways of the land, of *their* land, starting with the bedrock itself. Then might come the nature of seeds, and the miracle of plant life, and how a boll became cotton and then the shirt on your back! She'd play in the dirt and inhale its riches. He even bought her a tiny pair of boy boots.

But Bee would have none of it. Long after she could walk, she gripped their hands when going outside, as if facing the danger of a busy city street. Sunlight on her eyelashes made her fuss and squint. Breezes got hair in her mouth. Once, with hope, Abrams saw her lift a pinecone from a decorative tray and rotate it for several seconds. But that was it. Unlike other children she possessed no interest in animals, only commenting, once she had the words, on their smell.

"Peee-yooo," she'd say in the buggy behind the horse, waving her hand over her nose.

Pee-yoo? Where did she—?

And later, "Betty's had Winter's Fairy since she was a little girl." This was when, apparently, Bee decided that she could tolerate the odor of horses enough to want one for herself. "And she had seven more before him."

"Does she even ride that ridiculous thing?" asked Abrams. By then he'd grown a beard and was plucking at a whisker that was longer than the rest. He'd seen Betty Luben with that horse exactly once, in the Quitman Independence Day Parade, its mane matted with a mess of ribbons.

"Every day," said Bee. Right. Every day.

What did Bee love? She loved the closed doors, the locked cabinets, the thinnest edges of gold. He'd cleared the hallway of its garish trinkets, only to have Bee fixate on the one remaining table with the single glinting knob, reaching up to the refractions inside. "There's a rainbow in here!" she would yell. She'd sit on her mother's lap at the mirrored vanity, dunking her hand into a jar of rose-scented cold cream, while Mary scraped her smearings back onto the lid. Bee yanked out every drawer to squeal at the long pearls, clinking necklaces, and brass-handled hairbrushes that they'd stored.

"Mother! Wear this!" she'd said, laying on Mary's shoulder an oversized, lotion-smeared, amethyst broach in the shape of a poodle.

"Oh, sweetie," Mary said, prying the broach from her fingers. "I would never wear that."

This is not to say that Bee was a creature of innate refinement. She was not. She had knock-knees atop her spindly legs, which she balanced in heavy-bottomed buckle shoes. She was forever stomping up and down the stairs with the grace of Frankenstein's monster, even when people were trying to sleep. Over time she grew worried about her burly red hair and attempted to tame it on the ironing board, laying her cheek sideways while her free arm grabbed for the smoking iron on the stove.

Abrams did feel a little guilt. She did not have the nanny, the night-nurse, the newest hats, the fashionable shoes. They took holiday on an island off of South Carolina instead of France, staying with cousins instead of in hotels, with no white-gloved porters or packaged soap. And when the other girls returned, speaking of *brioche* and *pain au chocolat*, Bee looked newly worried, with even more things to learn. She begged Abrams for a detachable lace collar, a single beaded pendant—anything, *anything* to lay across her plain brown dress. Her anxiety grew a sharp point, like a unicorn. "Doesn't it hurt your hair to wear it like that?" she once said to Mary, eyeing the pulled bun that she'd preferred since becoming a mother. Mary reached behind her head to touch it, looking wary and appalled. "It suits me just fine," she said. Bee explained that she preferred the gently unfurling locks of the girls at St. Agnes, especially those of Cindy Fackenweather, who really had a sense of taste.

"I worry," Mary said one night in bed.

"I know," said Abrams.

"We shouldn't have sent her to that school. It just made it worse."

"We don't know that," he said, though he suspected she was correct.

The theory that his wife turned over in the middle of the night was that they ought to have either spoiled her outright or deprived her without mercy. They had aimed too cowardly toward the middle; they'd been wishy-washy and uncommitted. Mary had her suspicions right from the start—did she not? Didn't she express her worries, when the girl was just a baby?

Abrams stared at the rafters. Beneath him the padded mattress seemed to be thinning under his weight. He was aware, through the stuffing, of iron girders crisscrossing his back.

Who knew why she was the way she was?

He could only control what he could control. That meant restructuring the commissary credit system, replacing the wooden creek bridges with steel, and ushering the whole of the Kensington acreage into the twentieth century. He personally oversaw the rebuilding project of the Sledge Negro School, its roof still half-missing since the hurricane of '35. In Memphis, the races respected one another; he had seen it himself. Whites didn't let Negro facilities become eyesores for everyone else.

And he would do something about the prison. He gathered his courage and ventured back into the woods, this time with a driverless vehicle, his groundskeeper, and the same coolie caretakers in their same wrinkled robes. If only they could tell him what they knew. The wheels ached over the swamp. He remembered the smell: the pines, the thick puddles. Unlike his childhood home that seemed to shrink after college, the forest felt larger, more engulfing,

The trees seemed to loom, blocking the sun.

There was the same crate of feed, its wood now splintered and weathered black. There was the same pails of food and water, greened over with chalky mildew. The building itself looked unchanged, save for its walls streaked with bird droppings and its bolts circled with flaky rust. There were dents from fallen branches and near the bottom, a dent outward, where a prisoner had lashed out. For once Abrams was grateful for Bee's distaste of the forest. Unlike him, she would never stumble into this place.

"How many are in there?" Abrams asked the groundskeeper.

"Twelve, I believe," he said. "Used to be twenty-two. They don't eat like they once done."

Abrams walked to the structure. Near his boots was the familiar trough, littered with stray yellow kernels. All those years ago they had crunched under his teeth, pressed his soft gums. "Do I just knock?" he said. The groundskeeper said nothing. The Chinaman shrugged; the Chinaman's wife hid behind his shoulder. "All right, then."

He knocked.

"Hello?" came Abrams's voice. He was unsure in what direction to point it. He felt like he was talking to the trees, to the air. "This is Abramaside Kensington. *Junior*, I should say. I'm visiting today. I happen to own the land on which this structure is built. Well, I didn't used to own it. It was my father's for a long time, and his father's before that, and so on."

There was no response. Were they asleep in there? The coolie woman frowned. But she said nothing.

"Well, anyway," Abrams shouted to the wall. "I've come to take a survey of this place. I want to make improvements to your situation."

No one spoke. Then a voice sounded from inside. "Coffee?"

Abrams froze. It was the voice of a man. It coughed, echoed, and spoke again. "You got coffee?"

The question filled him with panic. The coolie woman ran up, pulled a steel thermos from her bag, and lowered it under the wall. It disappeared and that was the last they heard from inside.

Back home, in his parlor, Abrams summoned the old groundskeeper. He was a white man, bent, with a face as long as a squash.

"I don't know much, I swear," he pleaded. "All's I know is to order two barrel's corn once a month, and to keep those coolies on the roll." That Chinese pair had the job for years. No one knew them in Quitman; they must have been chosen precisely for their foreignness. No one could ask them questions. "They're paid pretty good, you'd be surprised. Every day they do the feeding and the changing, rain or shine." Once they went in the middle of a hurricane, branches crashing all around, to bring the prisoners blankets and drill extra bolts into the roof and walls.

"Who ordered that done?" said Abrams, his voice shaking.

The squash-faced man blinked matter-of-factly. "Who else?" he said. Abrams did not know what to feel about this fact made plain: it was what he'd always sensed, but had no courage to confirm. He should have asked these things sooner, yes? Years ago! Why did he wait? But also thank God that he didn't. It was a pleasure not to know.

"Who's in there?" he asked. What did they do that was so terrible?

Rapes and murders, mostly. Maybe a couple grand thefts. But the groundskeeper had never seen the papers; he was only guessing. A deal had been made, probably long ago. There were no record books, no letters, no logs. Abrams himself had torn apart his father's office and found nothing.

The groundskeeper shook his finger. He knew they weren't from the Delta—they'd come from out-of-state. Louisiana, Tennessee, Arkansas, Oklahoma. It started—he *thought* it started—with Abrams's great granddaddy Kensington.

The China couple knew more, at least the day-to-day things, if they could speak it. They knew what each one liked: the youngest wanted a hand-held drum. The newest addition always wanted more blankets. The oldest enjoyed hot coffee, which the couple brought to him in a thermos. It was against the rules of the arrangement but they did it anyway.

How long had they been in there?

Twenty years, twenty-five years for the longest one. They were never getting out and they knew it. Hadn't put in anyone new in years, and it was a big ordeal when they did. Had to chain the prisoners to trees so they wouldn't escape, fifty feet apart. Same for a removal when one of them died.

Why was it a secret? Couldn't it have been just a regular Negro prison? The groundskeeper could not say. Somewhere along the line, it began to smell like a secret, and he guessed it stuck. "Never had to be told," said the groundskeeper. "I just knew."

But he couldn't give Abrams the pure facts. He didn't know; he wasn't there. "And don't go getting mad at your granddaddies or some such thing. They did it for you. They did it for your daughter. And those were different times, mind you. They ain't always had these luxuries."

"Connect me to the people in charge of this," Abrams told him. He expected someone to come to him, to finally explain it all. But he only received one anonymous letter with no address and no signature.

Dear Kensington Junior, it read. *By now you have likely heard of the arrangement between the Kensington estate and the county penal system.* It was three lines long; it explained nothing of the past. *We trust that you'll continue to carry out the settled terms, including the provision of monthly rations, ongoing maintenance, and personnel as needed.*

Included was a check, dated April 1938. So there it was: the payments. Eight hundred a month from the State of Mississippi, and where had it gone? The teacups, the mahogany, the imported Belgian crystal goblets?

Well, he would put an end to that. He would return his inheritance to where it belonged. Maintenance indeed.

In came the paved roads, for easy access through the forest. Electric wires that Abe ordered himself to power heaters in winter and fans in summer. A new food closet of insulated cedar, custom-built by a craftsman in Oxford. The original frame he left standing—it felt wrong to destroy completely what his great granddaddy had built—but rectangles were punched out to make tall windows. Triple-thick glass drilled with lines of dotted airholes: not enough to smell the pines, but enough to breathe. Even a toilet was installed, in an annex with an internal door, for privacy. Mary applauded him, said that he was finally righting his family's sins. Into an oversized truck bed went the shards of the old prison, where it was rolled from the swamp and gone for good.

All the while Abrams forbid the practice of chaining the prisoners to trees; instead he built a separate, temporary structure beside the original and housed them there. He even had the prisoners build part of the road themselves, roped together at the ankles. He imagined them enjoying for the first time some fresh forest air, the warmth of the sun on their faces.

Townspeople heard that Abrams was building a brand-new prison for Negroes. *The costliness!* they said. *I could use a second home myself.* Ugly telephone poles, thick as tree trunks, were sunk into the swamp and buttressed by wayward two-by-fours. Black wires were strung all the way from Crenshaw. It confused the birds. Probably one would get electrocuted. More than anything it was this sight that made the town uneasy—the lone cable looping along the pristine horizon, off to make sure some rapists were enjoying a satisfactory temperature. Was Abrams losing his grip? Knowing about this age-old prison did not ease the minds of Quitman; it only brought them new anxiety.

But Abrams didn't care. He wanted the truth out. He publicized news of the renovations himself, called the editor of *The Quitman Weekly*. "Kensington Junior Brings New Light to Old Jail," read the headline. There would be transparency; there would be unwavering scruples. And no more *jail* or *prison*—he would call it a penitentiary.

By then all the young people were full of strange new slang: this was *hep*, that was *mode*. It had floated down from colleges and boarding schools in the north. Abrams didn't know what a *saucebox* was, but it sounded obscene. They even had a new name for their home. No longer was it Quitman—they were calling it "Q County."

"How groundbreaking," said Abrams to Bee. "I suppose I'm just a geezer now, according to my own daughter."

"It's just a word," she said, sipping a teacup of coffee. "No need to make a fuss."

He had to admit that there was something *hep* about it. He called the sign-painter on the phone. "That's right," he said. "Just Q." A week later the final product was hung outside the prison: *Q County Colored Penitentiary.*

Despite all of this, he could not bear to bring his daughter there. "Where are you going? Can I come?" she would ask him, pausing from her piano lesson. Abrams looked down at his outerwear, his same old boots and cape. How could she tell that *that* was where he was going? All this urging and pushing, and now was the moment she wanted to join him?

"Not today, Queen Bee," he said. "Not a good day."

Why not?

He was proud of the prison, of the improvements he'd made. Yet something inside of him didn't want her to see it. "It's a long way, darling. And it's only business. You'd be bored to tears." He searched for something more. "Why don't you work more on that necklace you've been making? The one with the feathers? I'd love to see it when I get back."

"I don't want to work on that," she said. "I want to see the forest."*Couldn't she go with him? Please, daddy? Please?*

"I wish so, Bee. I really do." Bee was quiet. She turned back to the piano and banged out clashing chords.

The project was finished in fourteen months, just before Christmas. Abrams had a tree sawed from his property and propped up in the West parlor, where Bee and Mary adorned it with strings of popcorn and intricate paper snowflakes. Abrams fluffed the rug by the fireplace and they huddled around it, sipping spiced cider. Bee loved Christmas in all its ornament and sparkle.

Right around this time came the first escape.

It happened in the middle of the morning, after the daily feeding. They wouldn't even have noticed, if not for the trail of corn dropped accidentally outside the fence. Abrams himself didn't learn of it until lunchtime, when the Chinawoman came sprinting to his door, tripping on the ends of her robe. She didn't know the word for escape. "He go!" she screamed in Abrams' face, her eyes wind-whipped and frantic. "He go!"

The first priority was to organize city officials to apprehend him. But by Abram's fifth unanswered phone call, a team of Quitman men were already collecting rifles from the barn. Plawson, Matthews, Arlo, Todd Panette. "Should I stop them?" Abrams asked Mary. She chewed her lip. Then she said, "Let them do it. The sheriff's slow, and anyhow, they want to." The men filled their arms with ropes and knives. *What else?* they yelled to one another. Never had this happened before. Would they need baseball bats, a fishing net?

By afternoon tea all of Quitman County seemed to know. The phone in the hallway rang and rang, and Mary filled a notepad with messages and handed them to Kensington as he fielded visitors at the door. A reporter came, followed by a photographer. The County Commissioner himself called to express his concern. "Abramaside Senior entrusted a lot to you, you know," he said. His voice was elegant and as familiar as the shuffling of cards, the pipe smoke, the shells of peanuts. "I know, I know," said Kensington, feeling like a boy. His hand shook as he hung up. Something had to be done. He called up the groundskeeper and ordered him to suspend the prisoners' meals and close off the toilet annex. Then he called back the commissioner to inform him of this swift action, but was forced to leave a message with the secretary.

Upstairs, in the master bedroom, Abrams searched the horizon. A convict. Hiding on his land, eating his berries, sipping his creek water, pissing in his patches of grass. Kensington watched the search team moving through the forest, their lanterns bobbing like fireflies among the trees.

Around eleven o'clock they came staggering back. They'd found him, they said. But something about him was strange. The prisoner had been walking in plain sight, down the middle of the main road, moonlight illuminating him. He wore pants torn at the ankles, a hat over his eyes, and carried a walking stick, as if he were only a man on a leisurely stroll. The hat at night: that's what gave him away. The search team pulled the coolies from their shacks by their long braids to identify him. They were drunk and jabbering in their native tongue, upset about losing a prisoner. But eventually the couple insisted that they could not verify the man, because they only knew the prisoners by the sounds of their voices.

They approached the man with a horsewhip. "Speak," they told him. He would not speak.

Striking was not the word for it. Lashed? Licked, whipped,

cut? Broke. It broke open the skin.

And so they broke him: one diagonal across his chest. He fell forward on his hands. They broke him on the shoulders. They broke him across the calves, where his skin was exposed. They broke him until he cried out, and the Chinawoman's eyes startled. The couple nodded their heads, Yes. That was a cry they knew.

The groundskeeper relayed the whole scene for him, in the parlor with a glass of iced tea. He had a lively story-telling style, all hands, which Kensington regretted now. "That's enough," he told him. Mary paced the floors and sent Bee back up to bed.

By one in the morning, thankfully, all was settled. *The Quitman Weekly* printed its next issue a day early, the headline in all capitals: KENSINGTON RAPIST FOUND & RETURNED. RELIEF COMES TO COUNTY.

In town, at events, people seemed nervous in his presence. He made jokes. They laughed—at first tensely, then genuinely. "That's not a *trapdoor* you've got here, is it?" he'd say, tapping the floor. "Are you on a *wild goose hunt*?" He felt the need to display his assured command, much to the surprise of Mary, who never before could lure him to parties. Now he wanted to attend more than she did. "Another debutante?" she said, eyeing a new invitation. Since when did he care for some neighbor's cousin's daughter's coming-out? He invited the commissioner to dinner, who said Thank you, That would be nice, he would get back to him with possible dates. Kensington waited.

Altogether the matter died down, and the *Weekly* turned to matters of crop counts and engagements and the upcoming county fair.

Then it happened again. This time in the middle of the night. Same man, different stretch of road. Same leisurely walk. He was not hiding, and that's what was so curious. Who was he, anyhow? He went by Hammond, the groundskeeper reported. He enjoyed coffee, he knew how to whistle. Some worried, seeing as he was the oldest, that he might be training other prisoners to do the same. But that was all suspicion; tense minds leapt to the worst.

An alarm system was developed: The China guards, upon discovering Hammond missing, were to bang on a metal pail with whatever they had—a wooden spoon, a fork. The guard would run. And when the clanging came within earshot of whoever heard it, that person would bang his own pot, as would the next man and the next after him, until the clanging arrived at the Kensington veranda and the men readied to chase the prisoner down. Everyone knew to leave their houses and gather their loved ones, to make sure that all were accounted for.

Each time Hammond escaped (and it was five times now: twice in winter, once in summer, and twice around Easter), the same men went scouting into the woods and the fields, searching outhouses, releasing dogs, peering under beds and floorboards. They stopped every Negro in the road, asked them to speak, and pointed their guns. The sharecroppers refused to work the fields until safety was restored—an entire day's work lost. The ad hoc team became more practiced, and soon their sons joined too. But each time they caught Hammond, he was not hiding but leaving, discovered no more than ten miles away and in plain sight, like any ordinary traveler. He did not even go quickly. They would net him and cuff him and simply drag him back to the penitentiary. It was too easy. He wouldn't say how he'd managed to escape, and neither would the other prisoners, despite the whippings.

Some said that it was precisely Kensington's meddling, his foolish wish to give those prisoners a better life, that caused the whole problem. Those long days of clearing the forest path, that taste of industry and modern machinery—it had given them time to memorize the trees, to make plans. But more importantly, it gave them desire. They were better off forgetting the world outside altogether. Give a man a spring and he'll only want an ocean.

But the waves of progress must move forward. He reprimand-ed the China couple—they, too, needed strict supervision. He prom-ised more complicated locks, reinforced doors, and higher fences. He poured his savings into the task. For the first time, Kensington began tracking his accounts himself, trying to make sense of the ledgers late into the night. Eyes stinging, he'd remove his glasses and roam about the East Wing, survey the fireplaces disappearing perfectly good logs to an audience of no one.

"I wonder if we really need a taste of the tropics every which way we go?" he said to Mary in the drawing room.

She put down her sewing—another item for Bee's trousseau. Bee was helping her, embroidering the edges of a future table run-ner. "Speak for yourself," said Mary. "We're perfectly comfortable." Something about her was different too—she no longer gave and received, but instead seemed to absorb. What she gave was advice, arguments, declarations.

"I'm just trying to be mindful of the sweat that people put into that tree-cutting," said Kensington.

"Will you two stop it?" said Bee, squeezing her embroidery. "I've just about had it." Her cheeks were flushed, but with her new-ly-discovered rouge she looked that way all the time now.

And then there was the matter of Bee's coming out. What had long been envisioned as a simple affair—some finger sandwiches, a spigot of punch—needed revision. Overdue, under planned—through all the distractions of the past year they'd delayed it, not occurring at year sixteen like everybody else but instead at the rapidly expiring age of seventeen. Bee was terribly embarrassed. Month after month she endured the explosively adorned houses, the golden sashes draped over chandeliers, the platters of ham and heaps of grapes, the individual petit fours. That custom-written song played on a lute as Cindy Fackenweather, glitter-eared and sprouting from her thousand-layer gown, descended her spiral staircase. The questions that day: When is yours, Trixie? We didn't miss it, did we? *Soon,* was her nodding reply. And she flew home to her room through slamming doors, relaying the whole ordeal through coal-streamed tears.

He felt the need to make it up to her.

There would be a theme. Horse shows, steeplechase, jumping rides, derby. Though Bee hadn't attended any such event, the magazines taught her everything; plus, it had the added advantage of being fancier and more distinct than the themes of all the other girls: Summer Picnic, Holiday at the Beach, Easter Parade, *The Jungle Book*. In came the planned drawings for saddle-shaped cakes and invitations letter-pressed with miniature horseshoes. Every guest was to come in equestrian attire, or as their favorite racehorse name—Winter's Fairy, as one example. For party favors they'd be given wine-colored velvet helmets (the overall theme color being purple).

"Doesn't somebody make fake ones?" said Mary, squinting at the bills. The young men would come as famous jockeys, whatever that meant. Only Bee knew.

"We won't have anything left for her trousseau," said Mary.

"Could we have a real horse?" said Bee.

"No horse," said Kensington. He kept his face serious. The truth was he had already planned to buy her one, not as a prop but as a present—an elegant white mare to reveal at the party. "But how about a dance? We could clear out all the chairs, get dance cards printed."

"Truly?" said Bee, her darkened eyebrows rising, stunned.

"We only debut once in this lifetime," said Kensington. "Don't we?"

Every offering on his part seemed both to excite and worry her. Did she feel odd, not having to beg and plead? To have it given freely?

As an extra-special treat—unheard of, unthought-of—it would be a sleep-away party. Boys on the first floor, girls on the second, and five mother supervisors stationed among them. Twenty-eight girls, twelve boys: ninety-three total guests including family and friends. He'd had the idea after discovering a purple-inked note on her bedroom desk, addressed to a boy, somebody named Brandon. *You ought to give my handkerchief back. THIS INSTANT.* With a tiny drawn flower she'd signed her name: "Trixie Kensington." Trixie? Who was this vulnerable, adorable person? She must be honored.

Kensington summoned Maggie to be in charge, and she set to work. Up came the boxes from storage, the lids of trunks flung open, an outpouring of silk and paste jewels and gold candlesticks. Everybody thought that Bee would burst.

"I never knew!" she gasped, burrowing her face in an armful of translucent linens.

He would invite the commissioner. Yes, yes. A stupendous party, unforgettable. What a feat those Kensingtons could put together! On their famed estate, in all its glory.

Every closed door opened. Closets cleaned, windows washed. Sheets were snapped and fitted over beds. Bee ran from room to room, new strings of beads swishing from her neck. *We had all this?* she said. *All this, all along?*

"Look what Bee wants me to wear." Mary grinned into the parlor where Kensington was signing a clipboard. On her head was a gigantic hat of spraying feathers. Bee came running behind her, concerned.

"I know that hat," said Kensington. "That's my grandmother's."

Mary laughed. "Isn't it a riot? What a ridiculous thing." She balanced it with one hand, looking at her husband and her daughter.

"It's very mode," said Bee. "It's fun."

"Fun if you're a circus clown," said Mary.

"I think you should wear it," said Kensington. Mary blinked at him.

"Oh, would you?" said Bee. "You really ought to. You should."

"It's becoming on you," he said, and Bee gleamed.

Mary removed her hat and crossed her arms. But Kensington didn't care. His daughter was gazing at him like the sun rising from the earth.

On the morning of the party, Kensington went upstairs to offer the new young lady a platter of croissants. A hired attendant was unwrapping her hair from rollers and coating it in a slick substance that she warmed in her palms. She pinned each section against Bee's skull.

"I thought you liked your hair down?" said Kensington. "In waves?"

"Did I say that?" She smiled at him. "I would never say that."

Stacked white cane chairs were wheeled over smooth floors where the rugs had been pulled away. Mary wound candlesticks with lavender taffeta and positioned them all over the ledges and the banquet table. Maggie directed the caterers on how to place the dinner plate down first, then the salad plate on top, lined up so you could see both their matching, plum-colored rims.

Kensington snuck off to the barn to prepare the debutante present himself. The white horse whinnied when she saw him, as if even she knew what was coming. On her head he attached a massive violet-colored bow. He nearly skipped across the yard and back up to the master bedroom, where he put on his finest suit, the one he'd gotten married in nearly twenty years ago. And when the first doorbell rang, his heart rattled like something bursting from its cage. He descended the staircase and took his proper place in the greeting line between Ms. Margaret and his wife, who wore no hat and would not look at him. Bee herself would wait upstairs until the proper unveiling.

Here they came—a train of frills and top hats, long coattails and shawls. Colognes and perfumes of every make and era—dusty lilac, peach, cedar, crushed rose—hazed together in a nostril-itching mess, as Kensington held his breath to stop himself from sneezing. All those little girls he'd known had their faces painted and nails lacquered and hair polished. When he took their gloved hands, they curtsied—real curtsies! He hadn't seen a girl curtsy since he was a boy. Altogether it felt like another time, another century.

He could not discern what was jockey-esque about the boys, but no matter. One extended his hand and introduced himself as Brandon Tortebaum.

"Brandon," said Kensington, gripping the boy's hand a moment longer. "I see." He was red-haired and possessed the flush of strength and future handsomeness. Kensington smiled to himself. His daughter chose well.

In the edge of his vision, the commissioner was being inched along in his wheelchair. Kensington bent to greet him. "Good afternoon, Commissioner."

"Are those your combines out there?" said the man, holding fast to Kensington's fingers.

"Why, yes," he said, startled. "They're full steel, shipped last month from Ohio."

"How much do they pull?" Kensington told him, the commissioner leaning forward to hear. The man grinned. Kensington could hardly believe it, this grin.

"Commissioner," he said. "May I show you to the head of the table?"

"Don't be silly," said the man, dismissing the idea with his hand. "I'd prefer a seat by you, if I may?"

Kensington lit up. "Of course," he said, heart flittering, and sent for the seating cards to be rearranged.

A gong sounded—a deep bloom rising over the foyer. The percussionist from the hired ensemble had struck it—unnecessary for the upcoming musical set but nonetheless wheeled in for this moment. A hush came over the crowd, as they looked to the top of the stairs. Out from the dark archways stepped Bee. At first Kensington did not recognize her. She stood pin-straight. Her lips were a startling shade of burgundy. On her head was an enormous derby hat, shading her face alluringly. A hoop skirt of a thousand stacked ruffles drowned any evidence of her knock-knees.

The photographer flashed his bulb.

"Gorgeous," said the commissioner.

She was indeed. A woman now. Little Bee.

Trays were passed—cold scallops rolled with curls of watercress, fried corn cakes dipped in brown butter and sage. Bee descended the staircase and the crowd gobbled her up. Kensington closed his mouth around a corn cake and held it on his tongue, feeling its warmth, its savory and pleasant grit. This was turning out to be a wonderful party after all. More hors d'oeuvres! He sipped his bourbon and waved over another servant. "*Horse* d'oeuvres," Kensington joked, and both men laughed.

Dinner began: the grand banquet of roasted pig and orange slices and glossy mounds of greens. The commissioner was wheeled to his spot next to Kensington, his knees angled carefully under the table. The servants rotated around the table to spoon hot soup into individual bowls—what a classy touch!—when a faint rhythmic sound slid through the conversations. No. It couldn't be. The guests kept talking, then stopped to make out the sound becoming louder, closer. Kensington stared at his soup, the steam fogging his glasses. Please, no. Please. Please. Lord in Heaven: No.

They were already pushing back their chairs, abandoning their napkins to the seat cushions, scrambling to the East windows. There he was: the lone coolie sprinting from the dark line of trees across the wide green basin of the field, his arms extended and banging on that same tin pot with that same wooden spoon. He was running toward them, toward the house. Even after he saw them—after he saw that they saw him, knew the message was clear—he did not stop running and banging on his pot, his pant legs flapping behind him, eyes crazy. He did not stop until he reached the veranda and scrambled up the steps. Somebody edged from the crowd to offer an iced tea to his panting body.

There was no time to waste. The usual team hurried to fetch their rifles from the coatroom, dropped their top hats to the floor, and lifted every Kensington family rifle from their mounted places in the drawing room. They took ammunition. They took a set of whistles. The women helped load a utility truck, and then a stake bed, and even John Baylil's sedan. Every man young and old wanted to go. Somebody grabbed a net; a girl pulled a rose from her hair and tossed it into the truck. They worried aloud about how the cars would get through the woods. Amid the commotion Kensington hardly moved from his dining chair. Nothing was requested of him; nobody needed him. They paused in their sprints only to ask him one question: *Do you have any horses?*

They took the white horse.

They led it from the barn, its long legs and gigantic purple bow plainly in sight of the North Parlor window. They pulled off the bow, dropped it to the grass, mounted the horse's back, and rode away—that was when Bee couldn't take it anymore. She crumpled under the window and down into the layers of her dress, glancing only to look again at the ribbon abandoned on the lawn.

They tried to comfort her, draping their arms around her and brushing her hair behind her ear. One girl brought over a stray suit jacket and balanced it over Bee's sobbing shoulders. They reheated a cup of soup and fed her spoonfuls. When her cries subsided, a girl knelt on the rug and volunteered to reapply her mascara, direct-ing her to listen to the ensemble readying to perform. On the small stage the musicians squirmed in their vests, and tried to play but were now missing the violin, cello, and French horn. Only a lone percussionist and thin-breathed boy on flute tried to get through the planned order of songs, their faces worried and distracted, until Mary ran up to the stage and tried to lead them in a roaring march with her pencil-baton.

Thank God for Mary. She improvised a card game involving forks and spoons among the wreckage of the banquet table. She cracked jokes. She had the girls' wet-eyed attention. The Equestri-an Competition proceeded as planned. Mary stood midway up the staircase in her helmet and skewed knickerbockers, announcing the winners from a card. "Best Mane" went to Ida Florine, naturally. "Best Manners" to Sheila Horn. One by one they climbed the steps to receive their bright and shiny ribbons, to pause for the photog-rapher. The crowd clapped good-naturedly. "Best in Show" went to Beatrice Marigold Kensington, to nobody's surprise, her mother kissing her cheek that couldn't help but glow with pride.

Afterwards they settled around the snapping fireplace in the parlor, among the wingbacks chairs and puffy pillows, with an air of exhausted cheer. They unbent their knees, let their long arms flop across cushions. Kensington lowered into an armchair, watching. He crossed his legs and felt his muscles loosen and sink. He loved these girls, all of them; he was awed by their existence. He saw in them something he had never seen before. The fringed blankets, the cuddling: they loved it all. They loved being girls. They loved being the girls that they were.

Some time later a knock came from behind the front door.

They started and glanced at one another. Maggie rose to an-swer it. She disappeared into the foyer, unclicked the latch, and screamed.

Kensington ran out, and everyone rose to follow him. There, in the doorway, stood a stooped Negro man. His gray-haired head seemed to bobble on his skeleton. He leaned on a long stick with one hand, and in the other held a makeshift bag of tied cloth. His skin was withered but clean. His beard was white.

"Abramaside Kensington?" he said. His voice was streaked with gravel.

Kensington could not speak. "Yes?" he coughed.

"My name is George Clarence Hammond," he said. "I believe I'm the prisoner you's men are looking for." He had almost no teeth, just three lone flashes of yellow. He looked around at what Kensington saw too: staring faces, hands over mouths, long fingernails clenching frilled skirts. "Don't mean no interruption," he said.

Kensington fumbled with the bottom edge of his jacket. The men had taken all the guns. In the kitchen there were knives, some shovels in the tool shed—what else?

"I'll get right to the quick," said Hammond. His eyes fixed on Kensington, steady and unblinking. "I'm here to have you's release me from jail. You tell the jail people that they ain't having me back no more."

Kensington startled. He paused. "I'm afraid I can't do that. It's not in my power."

"Yes it is," said the man. "You own this land, your daddy done owned it and your granddaddies done owned it all the way back. You said so your ownself. Say what people say but it's your prison. You can tell them not to want me anymore."

"I can't—"

"Mister." The man insisted.

"It's not possible."

"Look," he said. "Years ago I did a bad thing. Real bad, and the Lord and me both know it. But it's been thirty-one years. I been counting the winters. I've served my right time. They's want me in there until I die, but thirty-one years seems time enough to me."

Kensington felt the many eyes behind him, felt their throats tightening. Somewhere Bee was among them, but he didn't dare look. He couldn't let her see him like this, amidst everything he'd hidden. "They'll kill you anyhow," he said. "If they can't jail you, they'll kill you."

"Mister Kensington." Hammond lifted his palm. "I ain't interested in a freedom that I got to keep running to. I ain't interested in being chased. Now I'm going to go down that main road, and take it all the way out of town, and I ain't never, ever, coming back, so why don't you call off your men and let me ride out in peace and you get back to your party?"

Kensington clasped his own damp hands. A fly buzzed over the veranda; he couldn't tell if the air was cool or warm.

Who could say what confusions were in his heart? Not him. He did not examine options, did not turn them in the light or consider their refractions. He did not weigh, did not measure. When life turned its gaze on you, it offered no such luxuries. It pressed a gun to your ear and clicked.

He let the prisoner Hammond go.

Somebody, somewhere, would catch the man—yes? He turned from the silent crowd, went to the parlor, and shut the door. He emptied all the bourbon into a glass and opened all the windows. He waited to hear gunshots. But they did not come.

At some point came a soft knock at the door. The slippers shifting on the floorboards told him it was Maggie.

"Please go away," Kensington yelled. But the doorknob turned.

It was Bee, standing in her crushed dress, nervously twisting the doorknob back and forth. Despite everything, she'd applied a fresh coat of lipstick, and had fixed her eyes so that they looked less puffy.

"Daddy?" she said.

"Oh, sweetheart!" he said, and opened his sloppy arms. "Come!"

She ran to him and heaved her arms around his chest, slumping her head onto his shoulder. Kensington smelled her perfumed curls and held her, grateful that she'd come to comfort him in this way. "Thank you, my love," he said, squeezing her.

"Daddy," she said again, quietly. "This is the worst day of my life."

The worst day of *her* life?

"I've waited my whole life for this party," she said. "But now..."

He pulled her off of him, stood her upright. He looked at her smeared, blinking face, searching for a sign that she must be joking, that she must mean something else. Her eyes squeezed up and she buried them in her hands. "Just look at me," she said. "I'm ruined."

Kensington let go of her. He crossed his arms. "Enough of this. All of it. Don't you bother me with your prattle."

She uncovered her wet face. "What?"

"Get out," he said. "Now you've made this the worst day of *my* life." She looked shaken awake, scared, but he didn't give a damn. She ran out and he relished the sight of her, hurrying up the staircase like that. Finally the respect from someone—anyone—that he had deserved this whole damn time.

Around eleven o'clock the men returned. The women rushed in robes to greet them, telling what Kensington had done. The sleeves of the men were torn and hung loose around their hands; seams gapped at the shoulders to reveal puffed white undershirts. Their mouths drooped, eyes half-closed. Even Brandon had his red hair blown up and matted in wayward patterns. They smelled of sweat and dirt and swamp, their fine cologne wind-whipped away. But they also smelled of anger and pride and simmering discontent. Mothers kissed and gripped them. The younger girls eased the jackets off their shoulders and offered to mend them. Years later, many would cite this night, this moment on the West Veranda at the Beatrice Kensington Coming Out, as the beginning of the Kensington family's fall from grace.

The men wouldn't look Kensington in the eye as they filed out the door—not from disdain but with a kind of boredom, a disinterest, a fatigue. Then the girls paddled to their rooms and shut the day behind them.

Kensington steadied himself on the banister and eyed the staircase, its solid lines screwing in his vision. He turned around. He did not want to go up there, back to where he had come from. Instead he shuffled to the room behind the staircase, orange embers still glowing in the fireplace, where he collapsed onto the chaise and fell asleep.

Something woke Kensington in the middle of the night. The fire had died, the candles had melted flat. He fingered the button-punctured cushions underneath him and realized that he was not in his bed.

He had woken to a sound: the rhythmic banging of metal once again. Yet another prisoner must have escaped to God knows where. Was he delirious? Was he drunk? He hoped he was dreaming and having a terrible nightmare. But he was not.

Then came the confused shouts of girls echoing through the house. *Who now?* they screamed. *Were the doors locked? Did someone get in here?*

Kensington stumbled off of the chaise.

The girls scurried down the staircase, hair flying, waves loose, nightgowns trailing. They puddled at the bottom, as the adults tried to calm them. Some girls wore slippers, some were barefoot. One carried a stuffed orange rabbit in her armpit. They held one another by the shoulders and looked into each other's eyes, as if to make sure they were really the people they thought they were. Eyebrows and eyelashes were revealed to be blond, translucent, nonexistent. Course pimples dotted their foreheads and their chins. *Are you all right? Yes, yes we are, we just woke up, we ran.*

Maggie stood on the staircase and frantically scanned the heads. "Where's Bee?" she whispered loudly. Her eyes were crazy; she was talking to herself. "Did you see her up there? Bee?"

The girls looked around at one another. But none of them were *her.*

Kensington ran.

He took two steps at a time, past Maggie, leaping, catching the banister. At the top he caught his breath and turned into the hall, where every door was hanging open like a wagging tongue. On the long rug, a crumpled slipper. Candy wrappers, a hair roller. A strange wind tunneled through the hallway and rustled the prize ribbons that Mary had tacked over the girls' doors: pale blue, violet, shades of pink. At the end was Bee's door, closed and quiet, her giant, showy white ribbon flapping down to the knob. He pushed the door open.

He knew at once that she was not in danger. The window was shut, the curtains still, but more than anything he knew by the air, the atmosphere, the perfumes and the magazine cut-outs over the wallpaper and the straight pins scattered on the bureau. All of it belonged to the rightful habitat of Bee. A hundred damp cotton balls littered the floor under her mirror, smudged with black and tan and ruby-red smears. The tools of removing her beloved make-up. Kensington grabbed his damp forehead, overwhelmed and relieved.

In the bed was the figure of his daughter. "Bee," he whispered loudly. But she didn't move under the patchwork quilt, the frayed ends of her hair poking out of the edge.

"Get up, Bee. You have to get downstairs. Now!"

He threw back the quilt and there she was, arms and legs in her nightgown and a fury of straw hair. She covered her face with her hands.

"Don't look at me!" she yelled.

"Don't look at you?" He didn't understand. At her bare face? At his own little girl? "Up," he said. "I don't have time for this. Up now."

He grabbed her arm and pulled at her bent elbow. But it was like the root of a tree, stuck, exposed but held fast to something so much larger underground. She would not remove her hands. She would not rise from this bed, she would not go down there, she would not show this plain face. Did she not want to be seen? Or to see herself, being seen? Not even by him—her father— who loved her no matter what she was.

Are You a Self-Identified Black Woman?
by Krysten Hill

Are you eligible to partake in academia? Question your acceptance
letter? Not writing the other perspective? Missing the point of
the assignment? Do you get Tarantino's postmodern intention?
Are you misunderstanding the function of Flannery O'Connor's
Negroes? Do you wonder if your colleagues are looking for
the competent color in the room? Are you the only one in the room?
A performance of soft shoe? Are you inventing privilege?
Are there any side effects? Do you self-isolate? Self-medicate? Suffer
from heavy sighing, eye-rolling, weight loss, friend loss, hair loss,
laugh loss, self loss, loss loss, silence? Did a doctor call your wounds
superficial? Did a stranger spit at the sight of you in a dress you
thought you wore better than the smile you wiped off with
the back of your hand? Did you spit back? Did a man at the bar say you
were *too ugly to rape*? Did you imagine what the sound of your glass
against his head would make? Are there problems with your resting
bitch face at parties? Is your face ever really resting? Are you tired
of being cute because you're trying not to be threatening? Do you
wonder if white girls' tears are worth more than yours? Compare
your heaviness to someone lighter? Was there ever a time when
the faces of magazines pushed against the walls of your stomach
when you were thirteen, sixteen, twenty, and your finger belonged to
your tongue? Did you try to purge the light from haloed faces?
 What did you face instead? Pieces of undigested meat? Were you
ever a phase? Something he had to get out of his system? Do you
remember the clamp of a white boyfriend's jaw on your thigh? Do
you remember what he called you when he took you from behind?

Do you cry when you think of the way he treated your love like a bad taste? Did he spit you out? Do they ask why you don't write about your joy? Why is it hard to trust them with that? Do you wish they'd stop telling you to write around what goes through you? Wish your voice as strong and dismissive as your mama's swollen laugh? Do you cry often in this city? Do you cry at the noise of young girls swinging their lamp-lit lives against the sway of train cars, stringing their racing voices inside you? Do you cry because there are those who want to bury these breaths, smother these names, this anger, this pain, call it *defensive, non-compliant, threatening, unresponsive*?

Do you cry at the sight of other black women with their hands up?

MARCUSE ON THE MTA

EXCERPTED FROM *HERBERT MARCUSE, PHILOSOPHER OF UTOPIA* BY NICK THORKELSON

WHILE MARCUSE'S IDEAS WERE CHALLENGING TO HIS PEERS, HIS **STUBBORN UTOPIANISM** EXCITED A YOUNGER GENERATION OF REBEL WOMEN.

AMERICAN FREUDIANS ARE FIXATED ON **OEDIPUS** — THE EXEMPLAR OF **GUILT** AND **PATRIARCHY.**

BUT **THIS GUY** WANTS TO TALK ABOUT THE **PRE-OEDIPAL** NURTURING **MOTHER** RATHER THAN THE PHALLUS-WIELDING **POWERFUL FATHER.**

AND LISTEN TO THIS: "THE ORGANIZATION OF SEXUALITY MIRRORS THE ORGANIZATION OF SOCIETY, SO A **STRIKE AGAINST** ONE NECESSARILY **UNDERMINES THE OTHER!**

THE PERSONAL IS POLITICAL, YOU MIGHT SAY.

EROS and CIVILIZATION

HERBERT MARCUSE

MARCUSE RETURNED THE COMPLIMENT WHEN HE ADDED A "POLITICAL PREFACE" TO THE BOOK'S SECOND EDITION IN 1966.

BY NATURE, THE **YOUNG** ARE IN THE FOREFRONT OF THOSE WHO FIGHT AGAINST A CIVILIZATION THAT STRIVES TO SHORTEN THE "DETOUR TO DEATH."

THE FIGHT FOR EROS IS A POLITICAL FIGHT!

NO HUMAN BEING IS ILLEGAL

DISARM HATE

BLACK LIVES MATTER

PROTECT WATER

PUSSY GRABS BACK!

India

by Vi Khi Nao

You defecate
Then you get raped
Or you get raped
Then you can
Defecate
To defeat rape
All women in
India should stop
Eating
Samosa, biryani, chicken tikka masala, tandoori lamb, roti, pani-
    puri, chapatti, jalebi, dosa, palak
paneer, naan, chana masala, keema, papadum, pav bhaji, raita,
    korma, pakora, vindaloo, shahi
paneer, laddu, dal makhani, kheer, idli, dhokla, rasqulla, ras
    malai, sambar, aloo gobi, khichdi,
chole bhature, vada pav, sheer khuma, rogan josh, hyderabadi
    birjani, modak, vada, kulfi,
sabudana khichadi, or any food that will compel women to defe-
    cate
Frequently,
Habitually,
Routinely,
Repeatedly,
Regularly,
Recurrently,
Continually,
And, specifically as in customarily

Meanwhile
Men in India
Could continue to eat
And continue to defecate
Naturally
Fearlessly
To avoid waste
Of toilet paper
They should use
Women's toes

Faces hands sleeves breasts hair
To wash away
Feces
Still clung
Tight to their
Male emporium

Author's note: For a year or so, each day I tried to google "World
News" on my phone browser. I believed it was Chrome. Each
day I read the world news and for awhile, "rape" was pop-
ular in India. One day, I read about girls and women being
raped while defecating. India's hygienic infrastructure, in
some areas (urban and rural), don't provide public or private
restrooms for their inhabitants. I wrote quite a few poems
and "India" was born in response to my daily visit of world
news that have been fashioned for my Google Chrome pal-
ette. I wonder what kind of poems I would write if I had used
another browser for my daily research.

Born Here, Freed Here

by Sari Boren

*"I was born a slave on a plantation in Franklin County, Virginia . . .
My life had its beginning in the midst of the most miserable, desolate,
and discouraging surroundings."*
—Booker T. Washington, *Up From Slavery*, 1901

The landscape at the Booker T. Washington National Monument
has a nostalgic beauty. A portion of the original slave planta-
tion, now a living-history farm, rolls out green and lush, the recon-
structed historic outbuildings picturesque against the trees and the
small tobacco plot kept farmed for interpretive, educational pur-
poses. The bucolic landscape of Washington's birthplace is a kind of
illusion, however. A trick of time. Absent the past's enslaved work-
ers, the picture-postcard views distort the site's legacy, the very
reason why these acres have been preserved. A visitor who drove
to this National Park past the nearby strip malls and gas stations
might think this wasn't such a bad place to live and work, here in
these green fields. Maybe this wasn't the worst place to be trapped.
    Look at that vegetable garden with its rough handmade fence and

those chickens scratching in the dirt, and there, *oh my god*, the adorable authentic heritage lambs.

Even the recreation of the twelve-by-sixteen-foot cabin where Washington's family lived can belie the daily misery and degradation of slavery with the old-timey charm of its hewn log construction. You must step inside to discover the absence of the most minimal makings of a home: no beds, no dressers, no cupboards. These were not necessary in the absence of comfort, extra clothes, or ample food.

At the Booker T. Washington National Monument, the National Park Service staff decided they needed a new exhibit for the visitor center, as a deliberate counterpoint to all this loveliness. I was hired as the exhibit's content developer and writer.

My design team colleagues and I were charged with interpreting the first nine years of Washington's childhood on this farm, where he was born and lived in slavery with his mother, brother and sister—and where they were all freed. That's the reason this site has been preserved. Of course, if every child enslaved were memorialized on the land where they toiled, the National Park Service would be managing a huge swath of the southern United States from Virginia down to Florida and across to Texas. We interpret this site because Washington, born enslaved, accomplished more with his life than most of us born into freedom ever will.

Even though I'd already worked on dozens of exhibits, I worried, as usual, about getting the story wrong. Not factually wrong. I had plenty of experts to guide me. Narratively wrong.

Getting it wrong for the school children and the Civil War enthusiasts, for the tourists collecting stamps in their NPS passports and for the heirs of white supremacy. For the Civil War apologists and the descendants of the enslaved.

Even the most well-intentioned history exhibit is a reduction, by design. A distillation from complexity. We can't fit a book-length biography into an exhibit of only 500 square feet, and wouldn't want to. We must consider not only the limits of physical space but of visitors' attention—standing, reading, walking, corralling (hungry) kids—and how to fashion for them a compelling and focused narrative from the chaos of history.

And yet, the challenge is that we need to open up, not reduce, the stories of slavery. For too long these accounts have been obscured by racist-driven neglect and the supremacy of Confederate heritage, even at the National Park Service.

" . . . wherever people act upon the idea that the disadvantage of one man is the good of another, there slavery exists." —Washington's "An Address on Abraham Lincoln before the Republican Club of New York City," 1909

Twenty or even ten years ago you could visit a National Park Service Civil War battlefield site and never know that slavery was the primary cause of the Civil War. You could learn the minutiae of battlefield tactics and strategies, the numbers of dead, and the litany of their gruesome injuries, without ever confronting the question of what they were fighting and dying for, and why the states had gone to war against each other in the first place.

This oversight was originally a legacy from when the country's War Department managed most military parks. The focus on military interpretation continued when the sites were transferred to the National Park Service in 1933. But that's certainly not the only reason why this omission continued for over sixty years.

Within several years of losing the war, former President of the Confederacy Jefferson Davis embarked on a remarkable revisionist campaign, asserting in the pages of his excessively long memoir and from the stages of his lecture tours that the War for Southern Independence, of Northern Aggression, of the Late Unpleasantness, was *not* fought over slavery. No matter that many of the southern states' declarations of secession named the preservation of slavery as their reason for leaving the Union. As just one example, Mississippi's declaration of secession gets right to it in the second sentence: "Our position is thoroughly identified with the institution of slavery—the greatest material interest of the world." This document goes on to use the word "slave" or "slavery" six more times.

After the war, the freed people of African descent, now legal citizens rather than property, were still oppressed and were vastly outnumbered and outflanked in the battle to record a version of events. The newly freed and even those who had been free but not fully enfranchised had thousands of stories to tell about slavery and the war, but they didn't have Davis's platform.

Well into the 20th century, white scholars dismissed the historical value of slave narratives for being "inauthentic" and "biased." Historian David Blight has described how post-Civil War historians of American slavery "did not acknowledge that slaves left any legitimate testimony on the character and meaning of their own lives." Even the foundational American memoir *Narrative of the Life of Frederick Douglass* was out of print for nearly a century until Harvard University Press published a modern edition in 1960.

Only by the end of the 20th century did the National Park Service, prodded by Congress and its own interpreters and historians, start to question whose histories it was choosing to carry forward and whose to leave behind. A report from the 1998 Conference of Battlefield Managers described a new direction for interpretation at Civil War battlefield sites:

"We have an inclination to tell the story of the literate, the enfranchised, or the landed—those whose thoughts and actions are generally recorded in the historical record. We do magnificent re-source-based interpretation of the use of antebellum manors by armies during the war, but little of the owners, slaves and servants who peopled and operated those sites prior to and during the war. . . . The result: interpretation that is biased racially and socio-economically."

I read about an NPS superintendent who gave a speech in which he "mentioned that slavery 'might' have been a cause of the Civil War." The public response revealed that not all Americans are pleased at the National Park Service's shift in interpreting the war. Within a few weeks of the speech "1,100 cards and letters were sent to the secretary of the interior demanding that [the superintendent] either resign or be fired."

Imagine, more than a thousand American citizens flourished a bitter pen because a park superintendent dared name slavery as a possible cause of the war. Even though the National Park Service now definitively and repeatedly names slavery as the national crime that tore the country apart, the desperate scrabble to reframe America's 19th-century self-portrait is relentless.

" . . . my whole life has largely been one of surprises. I believe that any man's life will be filled with constant, unexpected encouragements of this kind if he makes up his mind to do his level best each day of his life--that is, tries to make each day reach as nearly as possible the highwater mark of pure, unselfish, useful living." —Up From Slavery

Washington's exhortations of self-reliance and forgiveness were, I'm sure, a balm to the white folks nervous about a black man so damned articulate, so ambitious on behalf of his people and so convinced of the mutual benefits of a racially integrated America.

Washington transformed Alabama's Tuskegee Institute, formerly the Tuskegee Normal School, into one of the premiere schools for educating black citizens, many newly freed, in the post-Civil War years, and was conciliatory with the white power brokers and philanthropists who supported Tuskegee. He promoted an economics-based approach to black equality, which put him at odds with other African-American leaders such as W.E.B. Du Bois who pressed for political equality and legislative redress.

Washington knew the dangers of infuriating a white majority. His fellow citizens in Tuskegee's Alabama carried on with burning black schools and churches, as if through fire they could destroy any evidence of a shared humanity with their black neighbors. He was certainly practiced, as were most African Americans, in hiding his true self from white people.

With the echoes of slavery rumbling through Reconstruction and Jim Crow, it's not difficult to appreciate why Washington would construct a public face. Even Washington's name was partly an invention, the title to his persona. Lacking a family name and believing that the newly freed should cast off their names from slavery, he chose the last name Washington, the name of the country's white father (albeit a slave owner), to stand in for the name of his missing father, a man he never knew.

Washington remained circumspect about the challenges of running a black school amid such hostility, and downright secretive about his private life. When Washington's first wife Fanny died at a fairly young age, his few public remembrances sound like slights in his overreaching to protect their privacy: "Perhaps the way in which Fanny was able to impress her life upon others most was in her extreme neatness in her housekeeping and general work." And when his beloved second wife Olivia also passed at a young age from illness, he couldn't express his feelings to his closest mentor, instead writing, "Few will ever know just what she was to Tuskegee and me. But I can not trust myself to write more now."

Even as he sought and achieved public celebrity to further his cause and fund his school, Washington buttoned up his angers, his longings, and his losses beneath his elegant suit coat.

The face Washington presented to wealthy benefactors was certainly not the one he considered in the mirror, scraping a blade across the white mask of his morning's shaving soap. He may have seen a man frustrated by the pace of change or exhausted from ignoring the daily slights suffered as a black man. Or maybe he saw a man disappointed in how little of himself he saved for his wife, or bemused with how much he was getting away with.

Was he startled again each morning not to see the eager sixteen-year-old Booker who arrived filthy and destitute on the steps of Hampton College after an arduous 300 mile trek, in possession of only his keen mind and determination to be educated? Washington alone knew.

Washington was a real man, yet he's twinned to a constructed historical character deliberately created by Washington himself. In his many speeches and books he strung together words as if he knew he'd be quoted in perpetuity, as if he were consciously sculpting the public persona Booker T. Washington to be immortalized in museum exhibits.

Is it enough to know Washington through his public face? He remains more like a character than an individual. A role model, rather than just a man. The historic persona overtakes the person. Perhaps that's what he intended all along: never to relinquish ownership of his true self.

* * *

At the outset of each exhibit project I speed-read as much foundational content as I can, as if cramming for an exam in a class I haven't yet taken. I pick the brains of museum staff during meetings and phone calls, worried that as the content developer (but not content expert) and propelled by the project schedule, I'll miss something and diminish the efforts of the larger exhibit team. The exhibit design process is a collaborative one, and our individual efforts tightly interdependent.

The exhibit designer configures and reconfigures the exhibit space, puzzling through different arrangements of thematic areas and exhibit elements, and the functional design of interactive exhibits, models, and object displays. The graphic designer creates the overall visual aesthetic, integrating imagery and text and often acting as a project's art director. The entire team, including the project manager, brainstorms and develops iterations of the interactive exhibits, and we pair with specialty subcontractors, such as media producers, as a project requires.

By the time I started on the Booker T. Washington exhibit, I'd already worked on several exhibits that interpret slavery. From talking to park rangers I learned that some visitors to historic slave cabins will voice a mild protest when the conditions of slavery are described as a unique burden. These visitors insist that their white ancestors also lived difficult lives in shacks similar the slave cabins; they too were impoverished with barely any economic mobility.

Until I learned about these visitor comments I didn't realize I'd have to explain in the exhibit text why slavery was worse than poverty. So I wrote about the unique nature of American slavery: that it was racial, lifelong, and passed down from generation to generation. Then, after describing the terrible physical conditions of slavery—unceasing labor, insufficient food and clothing, and brutal violence—I reminded visitors that enslaved people had no citizenship and no liberty. When they worked long hours under inhumane conditions they were putting food on someone else's table and clothing someone else's children. They couldn't protect themselves or their loved ones. Free black men were kidnapped and sold into slavery and enslaved women were raped with impunity. The laws of our country allowed children to be taken from their parents and sold like livestock.

I harbor a petty resentment that I must devote a portion of my limited word count to addressing this—that slavery was more terrible than some would like to admit, and was, indeed, not only the cause of the Civil War, but the worst aspect of America. The park staff and I make sure that those who protest, still, that the War Between the States was fought over "states' rights," will know that the rights the seceding states demanded were the rights to own, retrieve, torture, rape, breed, buy, and sell people of African descent.

I must also follow the Editorial Style Guide of the National Park Service for writing exhibit text. While *slave* is the common label for people of African descent who lived under the American laws of slavery, *enslaved* is better, according to the 2015 NPS Style Guide: "*Enslaved* acknowledges the dignity of a human being; *slave* is a non-person, property." For those who protest that this is nothing more than political correctness, think about it: if your parents had both died, would you prefer to be known strictly as *foundling* or *orphan*? If those parents of yours never married should you be forever labeled *bastard*? A "slave" is a person stripped of his or her personhood and identified only by the condition of slavery, imposed without consent.

The right words make the person visible within the experience. The preferred naming is: *enslaved person* or *the enslaved*. The park superintendent at Washington's site preferred *enslaved Africans* or *enslaved person of African descent* to emphasize both the racial component of American slavery and people's African heritage. It also made my task of adhering to strict word counts more challenging: *slave* is one word; *enslaved person of African descent* is five. Repeat that three times in a 75-word panel and 20 percent of my word allotment is taken. But that's the point, in a way. *Slave* is shorthand, it's incomplete. A slur, a diminution, an abbreviation of a person.

The National Park Service's stance on language usage keeps

evolving. While the 2011, 2013 and 2015 NPS Style Guides recommended *enslaved* over *slave*, in previous guides the words *slave, enslaved*, or *slavery* never appeared at all. The nuances of naming the enslaved were not addressed in Style Guides written fewer than ten years ago.

"I would permit no man, no matter what his color might be, to narrow and degrade my soul by making me hate him." — Up From Slavery

Born Here, Freed Here. That's the theme we created for the new exhibit. It's the elemental take-away. *Born Here, Freed Here* printed on the colorful banners that parade up the drive.

To draw you out of your cars and toward the entrance, we broadcast field songs from the visitor center. The melodies of longing rise and fall over the steady work rhythms, easing your shift in perspective to the plantation's past. Once in the lobby, the view of the farmland beyond the building and the distant squawks of the animals might beckon you out the back glass doors. But we hope instead to lure you down the hall to your left, towards a formal photographic portrait of a middle-aged Washington. He's standing in an elegant coat, his right hand tucked under his lapel and his left holding papers, a suitable portrait for one the most influential American public figures of the late-19th and early-20th centuries. The photo looms over an almost-life-sized bronze statue of the enslaved boy he once was, barefoot and draped in a ragged shift (a statue we inherited from the park's previous exhibit). We designed this paired display of the distinguished, celebrated man rising above his childhood self in slavery to pull you down the hall toward our new exhibit, and to illustrate Washington's declaration that the man he became arose from his experience in slavery.

Who is the Booker T. Washington in the exhibit at the National Monument? He is the boy Washington describes in his memoir, poorly clothed and often hungry. On the Burrough family's plantation he fetches water, weeds fields in the hot Virginia sun, and takes sacks of corn to the mill. He is the barefoot boy forbidden from learning to read, carrying the books of his slave holder's daughter to school, the place he imagines as his most longed-for paradise. He stands by the supper table in the Burrough's house, fanning away the flies as they eat their fill without regard for his hunger, and discuss their fears of black emancipation without a thought to his presence. He is a boy loved by his mother and siblings.

The adult Washington in our exhibit is the famous one: practical, assured, and tireless in his efforts. From his wretched childhood, he extracts what he needs and discards any bitterness that might hold him back. He is almost too good to be true. And yet no matter his masks, he was a real man.

So we let Washington speak to his own history. His memories form the spine of the exhibit and then we frame his memories with thematic areas that expand on the exhibit title: Born Here, Freed Here. Past the twinned portraits of Washington, you turn into the 500-square-foot exhibit space transformed with large, curved mural walls that create both a visual backdrop and a distinct path through these areas: Born Here, Lived Here, Enslaved Here, Dreamed Here, Freed Here, Remembered Here.

At each area, you'll first read a quote from Washington, describing his childhood on this plantation. You can then choose to read the exhibit text printed across the murals' custom illustrations depicting enslaved life. These 75- and 100-word text labels describe Washington's specific experiences in slavery with his family, and how these fit in the broader historical context: the South's economic dependence on slavery; the laws preventing enslaved people from being educated; the effects of the Civil War on the residents of Virginia plantations, blacks and whites; and how formerly enslaved Americans tried to started new lives after emancipation.

In a flipbook, you can turn pages to see copies of historic property inventories and census records that are paired with questions meant to provoke discussion: "Why were the 'negro' men, women and children listed in the plantation inventory and not in the census?"

Among the dozens of items inventoried in the 1861 plantation property inventory are:

Grind stone $1.50

16 fat hogs $128

1 negro boy [Bowker] $400

In the 1860 slave census you see Washington listed, unnamed, among the other enslaved people as:

Age 4, Male, Mulatto

But none of the enslaved are included in the same year's federal census, which counted only white people.

You can listen to audio dramatizations voiced by actors, based on Washington's writings. In one, you'll hear the dinner table conversation among the Burroughs family members from the perspective of young Booker, who is fanning the flies from their meal. At another audio station you'll listen to Washington's recollections of the moment of emancipation, while you look through a window to the very spot out back where the enslaved people heard they were free. You may be thrilled to hear Washington's actual voice in a recording of his speech at the 1895 Atlanta Cotton States and International Exposition.

Because the park wanted this exhibit to appeal to families and school children, we even designed seven interactives. This is a tricky business because we didn't want to trivialize the experience of slavery but to guide you to an empathetic imagining of a life enslaved. In the design of the interactives we tried to show the resilience of those enduring the terrible conditions of slavery:

People who were forced into brutal, constant labor still made efforts to care for each other. At the "Hard Choices" interactive we ask if you would take a chicken to feed your children, as Booker's mother did. And would you, as Booker's older brother John did, wear the scratchy flax shirt Booker described as feeling like "a hundred small pin points" until it softened enough for Booker to wear.

At the interactive "What If You Couldn't Read?" we ask you to sort tasks that could or couldn't be done by enslaved people who were forbidden from learning to read. While they couldn't write a letter, they could still learn, and could teach each other their lifetimes' worth of experiences: to plant, to harvest, to cook, to sew, to build, to sing, to pray, to remember. Short of book learning, the plantation's enslaved workers were often more knowledgeable about running the farm than the farm's owners.

Others were able to deftly to glean valuable information, such as the movements of the Union Army, by eavesdropping on conversations. At the "What's the News?" interactive, you can listen to audio snippets of conversations to try to piece together news of the larger world. As Washington wrote: "the man who was sent to the [post] office would linger about the place long enough to get the drift of the conversation from the group of white people who naturally congregated there . . ."

After emancipation, Washington built an extraordinary life. So we share highlights of his full life's journey, etching his later memories into elegant, free-standing frosted glass panels. And when you look up, you'll see Washington's inspiring quotes on a banner that curves overhead like the ribbon tail of a kite.

When you admire the former plantation's landscape, it is Washington, not us, who fills in the blanks, Washington who describes the roughness of his flax shirt, the ache in his hungry belly, the yearning of his unfulfilled desires.

"I have learned that success is to be measured not so much by the position that one has reached in life as by the obstacles which he has had to overcome while trying to succeed." — Up From Slavery

The park staff at the Booker T. Washington National Monument know very well that their landscape can work at odds with their primary goal of interpreting slavery. So in addition to the new visitor center exhibit, the park offers ranger-led activities, outdoor interpretive signs, an audio tour and, for special events, living-history actors — all which tell the vital, hidden stories of this place. Reconstructing history is not always about burying the bones; it can be a revelation.

The park has researched and laid stones outlining the location of the home of the Burroughs, the white people who owned the plantation, with its land, livestock and enslaved people, including Washington and his family. Here the park has peeled away the years to make visible the landscape's true face: its enduring power as an artifact of slavery and emancipation.

From Washington's recollection in his book *Up From Slavery*, we know that he and the other enslaved people gathered in front of the Burroughs' "Big House" the day a Union soldier arrived. The uniformed man stood on the front porch with members of the Burroughs family, and with only words from a piece of paper and the sound of his voice, backed by the law of the land, they were free.

Free men and women. Free boys and girls. Free families, if they were lucky enough to have survived slavery together. Free husbands and wives whose marriages were not recognized by law.

" . . we were told that we were all free and could go when and where we pleased. My mother . . . kissed her children while tears of joy ran down her cheeks. . . . this was the day for which she had been so long praying but fearing that she would never live to see."

You can stand there, as I did, as visitors do, in the short grass in front of the stones that mark the outline of the Big House, where the sounds of pigs snuffling in the nearby pen mingle with the muffled noise of cars from the road beyond. You can stand in the precise spot where these people gathered all those years and a world ago. You might feel, as I did, a shiver not from the breeze, but from imagining the words that changed everyone's narrative. When person-by-person, black and white, each life pivoted off that moment: slave owner to slave owner no more; enslaved person to citizen.

Any story about the past, public or private, is partly an invention. But it's a useful invention, a necessary one. We peel away parts of the narrative that don't hew to the theme and unveil those that have remain hidden too long, so that for a brief time we can settle on one particular story, in this place and time. Every act of historical storytelling is a type of revisionist history.

The Booker T. Washington exhibit shares with visitors a narrative that is nested within the one Washington created for public view, and which we, in turn, interpret in response to the shifting American narrative of slavery and the Civil War. None of these is constant. None is fixed. We bind the truths of the past, as well as we can understand them now, to the stories we need to tell.

| 197

Henry and Ralph

A Transcendentalist Rallying Rap for A Republic In Crisis

by Regie Gibson

Henry Thoreau

Henry Thoreau told civilization: *Yo' I gotta go cause I need a vacation*
So he went to Walden and he had a revelation
Wo! Most of us live lives of quiet desperation
Lo and behold another old quotation
seems to capture the essence of a modern vexation
It's like Thoreau knew that in the future
you and I would have to act
in radical ways to mitigate the sad fact
that: Because we gotta slave to keep our bills paid
Sometimes it seems our minds are kinda' ripe to get played
by the vultures of our culture only hoping to withhold us
from anything any deeper than *work while we scold ya*
Buy what we told ya pay what you owe
Uh, and we'll insure you get a debt you'll never get over

treating human beings like mere skin machines where the cash is
some sick profiteer's demographics
or puppets made of plastic molded and mastered
stretched thin as thread until bled dead and into caskets

We try to contrast it by coming off sarcastic
but because the situation we're facing is so drastic
many of us huff puff and snort stuff to get blasted

hoping to deaden the pain that seems everlastin'
but we find that action serves to make the masses act more passive
keeping our minds inactive to the plans of the fascists
who wanna keep separated by races, genders, and classes
cause that's the way you keep the status quos status as is

But   don't let 'em head fake you
shake and bake and back break you down to the ground
come around to clown and undertake ya'
You've gotta fight back! and my advice is:
Use whatever thing of beauty you got trapped inside
you as a weapon

Do ya dig!? (Audience Repeats: "Yes, We Dig")

Ralph Waldo Emerson

Ralph Waldo Emerson was a brilliant thinker
known to be the don among New England Transcendentalists
he thought we all should become self-reliant existentialists:
trust our very own experience
and not rely upon the pre-conceptions we've inherited
like socio-cultural, racial and political prejudice
beware of demagogic fundamentalists
dig the way Ralph Waldo kicked that 19th century rhetoric:

To be yourself in a world that is constantly trying to
make you something else
is the greatest accomplishment
Don't give up cause every artist was once an amateur
and your character is of more value than your intellect

and guess what for every minute you are angry
kid you gonna lose sixty seconds of happiness
        Though the purpose of life is not to be happy.
        But to be useful and have your life make some difference.

to do any of this
requires us to make mental shifts
toward a broader vision and then broader consciousness
and listen to that higher self within the one that insists

Love, play, chant, meditate and then dance, yo
sometimes you gotta let go and take a chance on
becoming more than they told you you could be:
a transcendent human being and not a human "bling thing"

this world can be an enemy whose mission be
to empty you of empathy, intelligence and energy
can come around to destroy what joy you got left
make you wanna give up your last breath

But don't let 'em head fake ya'
shake and bake and back break ya'
down to the ground come around to clown and undertake ya'

You've gotta fight back   and my advice is:
Use whatever thing of beauty you got trapped inside
you as a weapon

Do ya dig!? (Audience Repeats: "Yes, We Dig")

A Cairn by the Cabin

by Fred Marchant

Walden, 2018

. . . the asphalt parking
lot, our summer high
thick heat, and children
with towels, flip-flops,
popsicle Rockets,
red white and blue ice . . .
. . . how deep the hole
our country did fall
into while we slept
and how the dream
brought us locusts,
their whine the sound
of a someone strapped
to the table, cut open,
for the hoses and salt . . .
. . . impossible to say
where we stand now
on a path that circles
what HDT said was
the eye of God but
now feels like a corner
where a sparrow has
fallen from its nest
and looks up at us,
bewildered as we are. . .

. . . down in the mud,
leafy pools, shallows,
deep within alluvial
history, our truths
unfolding beneath us,
so he wanted to find
out if there was after
all some granite there,
something we believed in,
that held us together . . .
. . . He must have known
it was always tentative
ready to fall apart,
that we each would
have to believe enough
to build it over again
and that this is what
these stones are here for. . .

The Ghosts We Carry with Us

by Sebastian Johnson

"Now I know what a ghost is. Unfinished business, that's what."
— Salman Rushdie, The Satanic Verses

*I*n 1904, Rufus Lesseur was abducted by a group of vigilantes on suspicion of sexually assaulting a white woman in Marengo County, Alabama. Despite the lack of substantial evidence, a jury trial, or any conviction in a court of law, Rufus was lynched outside a makeshift jail in Thomaston, his body riddled with bullets. He was 24 years old.

In Montgomery, Alabama, about 100 miles from the makeshift jail that still stands, a new memorial has been erected to honor Lesseur and the more than 4,000 Americans who were lynched. It is the culmination of years of heroic work on the part of the Equal Justice Institute and its indefatigable leader, Bryan Stevenson. I traveled to Montgomery last week to attend the memorial's opening and to support the work of philanthropies fighting for criminal justice reform. What I experienced there could fairly be called a conjuring.

Ghost stories are deeply embedded in Southern culture. Enslaved people wove tales of "haints" or "spooks," restless evil spirits who afflicted the living. As with many elements of the culture that developed among enslaved communities, these stories served a dual purpose — to be connective memories to common practices stemming from West African spiritual traditions, and to pass on coded messages about the brutality of slavery, subjugation, and death. Black fear of spooks and haints became a well-known stereotype — one often portrayed in minstrel shows, vaudeville acts, and early cinema.

The masters had their ghosts as well, though they were of a different kind, reflecting the base fear that their sin could literally come back to haunt them as terrifying revenants — the angry souls of the enslaved dead, intent on vengeance. In some parts of the South, they painted the ceilings of their porches "haint blue" to ward off and confound these spirits.

Of course, the lived experiences of far too many black lives have been more terrifying than any ghost story, as the National Memorial for Peace and Justice and the Legacy Museum in Montgomery make stunningly plain. Stories of men and women stolen from faraway shores, tossed overboard and drowned, of vessels of death trailed by sharks across the Middle Passage. Stories of forced marches overland to places of horrific bondage and extravagant wealth, spurred on by the lash of the whip. Stories of sexual violence and degradation, pervasive and persistent and passed through generations, of fathers holding their children as chattel. Stories of shadowy figures clad in white, prowling the night in search of black prey. Stories of torture and terror, of caprice and cruelty, of murder without justice and truths buried beneath soil and roots. Stories that say to all, clearly, that to be black — and simply to *be* — is to be shadowed by Death astride a pale white horse.

Stories like that of Fred Rochelle, who was burned alive at sixteen years old in Polk County, Florida for the amusement of the public. Or of Henry Smith, lynched at seventeen in Paris, Texas before 10,000 men, women, and children. Or Robert Mallard, lynched near Lyons, Georgia for having the temerity to own a successful farm and attempt to vote.

These stories are the ghosts we carry with us, the specters of racial terror that followed black refugees up out of the South to visit them in the ghettos and prisons of the North. The stories that lodge in every mind, trauma encoded in genes and hardened in hearts. When I told my father that I was visiting Montgomery, his only reaction was fear — a bone-deep memory of water hoses and fire bombings, billy clubs and rough nooses. An instinctive terror that his only son might join the rolls of the haunted.

These stories are the spirits that haunt our public commons and private spaces, stir restlessly in places of commerce and industry, tread the quiet backwoods and creek beds. Montgomery, this city of ghosts, its streets walked by the children of slaves and the children of former slave-owners. Its elegant esplanade along the river, where once steamboats and barges disgorged thousands of men, women, and children considered property. And today, its museum to account for this dark legacy, built atop the site where enslaved people were held in pens.

What is a haunting? Many scholars, philosophers, artists — and a fair number of fabulists — have attempted to describe the phenomena. One theory, drawing on the ideas of 19th-century intellectuals and pseudoscientists, explains it as a physical impression of an emotional or traumatic event, projected and stamped on a place, playing in an endless loop like a tape recorder on repeat.

Perhaps, then, we should consider our own hauntings: the endless loop of brutality against black bodies caught on crystal-clear smartphone video; on grainy VHS tape; in black and white newsreel footage; in yellowing newspapers and photographs; in postcards and burnt bits of charred flesh taken as souvenirs; in daguerreotypes of scarred backs; in engravings that implore, "Am I Not a Man and a Brother?" This haunting of violence and hate, our birthright and inheritance, a shapeshifter of many forms and faces, will always be with us. We are possessed, in both senses — our minds and spaces suffused with white supremacy, wholly owned property of that ancient lie.

A possession requires an exorcism — a confrontation, an incantation, an appeal to a higher power to cast out demons.

That is what this memorial is. The facing of a shameful past and its dark tendrils that choke our present moment. The invoking of our ancestors' names, their blood crying for justice from the ground, as a talisman of protection. An act of memory to ward off future evil. An appeal to our conscience in the hope that, finally, a malignant spirit be laid to rest so that the nation might live.

aiding and abetting

by Fred Marchant

I could stand in the middle of Fifth Avenue and shoot someone . . .
--DJT, 2016

you want to replicate a Glock
so you let your
index

finger, maybe the middle
finger too, be the
barrel

and you flex your thumb
into a hammer,
lift

it up, bend it to cock it,
and close the rest
turning

your fingers into a grip,
the magazine spring-
loaded,

first round chambered,
so when you
squeeze

and make that pursed-
lips shooting
sound

you will see your hand
jump a bit to remind
you

next time you have to
aim a little lower,
ok?

Meeting President Obama:
A Farewell to Representation
by Elorm Avakame

One day last fall, at a small campus in the heart of New England, I stood on an arena floor no more than 20 feet from the front of the stage on which Barack Obama would speak. Hundreds of people stood on the floor around me. Hundreds more were packed into the arena seats around the floor. The air buzzed with anticipation—all the more palpable since none of us knew if, in our lifetime, another such moment would happen. Not just us meeting the most powerful man in the world. But that this most powerful man in the world would be black.

This is a truth of American history: People whose skin and ancestry caused them to be considered black were once killed for attempting to vote. Before that, they were killed for trying to teach themselves to read and write. Before that, they were killed for daring to think themselves deserving of freedom. Underneath this truth of history persisted a vicious untruth: that these people were less intelligent, less capable, less worthy of respect. This lie is dying, but it is not dead. I know it lives because whenever a picture of me in my white coat is circulated on the internet, I read comments from people who assume that I am a Harvard medical student only because I must have been selected over a more deserving student of another race.

All of these thoughts swirled through my head, rising along with the excitement of the moment. Shortly before the President emerged onstage, I noticed a college student standing just in front of me. His hair was like mine – cut close on the sides, long and curly on the top. Music was blaring, and his shoulders bounced with a recognizable rhythm suggesting that someone had taught him how to dougie. I wondered if this chance to see the President meant to him what it was beginning to mean to me. And then, when Obama was being introduced, I saw him turn with wide eyes to his two friends, also young men with curly tops and deep brown skin, and I saw all three of their faces awash in equal parts excitement and disbelief, and I knew.

For a few moments during the President's speech I stopped listening to what he was saying and just looked at him, trying to fully grasp what I was seeing. Here was a man who for eight years had occupied the most powerful position in the known world, who had commanded respect from ordinary citizens and dignitaries and royalty – whether they wanted to respect him or not. Here was a man who had done a job that some had always assumed was beyond what people like him could do.

In that moment a reservoir of pride welled up within me at the thought that this president had stood defiantly against the noxious fiction of black inferiority. All those who had presumed blacks to be of inferior stock would be forced to gaze upon his brilliance and political success and accept that they were wrong. This, I felt, is the value of a black president.

But as that moment faded, and the last fall of his presidency came to its winter, I had to concede that President Obama's tenure could not dismantle racist logic. Racism is impervious to facts;

it is not based in reality and cannot be undone by it. It can cast a black president as a rare exception to an otherwise still-relevant rule. It can link our nation's shortcomings to our president's blackness. Just as some children born during Obama's tenure have been taught that his achievements mean there is no limit to what black people can achieve, many others have been taught that America's present struggles prove a black leader can never be entrusted to make America great.

And even the question of what it means to have been represented by a black president is further complicated by the way that he often presented black people to the world. President Obama always seemed more comfortable publicly criticizing the archetypal degenerate "Cousin Pookie" for failing to vote than he did criticizing Democratic politicians for failing to earn Cousin Pookie's vote; more comfortable criticizing black mothers for feeding their children "cold Popeyes" for breakfast than criticizing a society that crushes so many black mothers under the weight of unthinkable poverty and then expects them to feed their children the balanced diet they can't afford; more comfortable scolding black fathers for community breakdown than scolding the United States government for entrapping so many black people in conditions that demonstrably lead to poor social outcomes. Maybe he felt he needed to play this role. Perhaps he thought trafficking in well-worn tropes of black dysfunction helped reassure whomever needed reassuring that he did not intend to be the "president of black America." Nonetheless, when he proclaimed that he would consider it a "personal insult" if black Americans did not turn out to vote for Hillary Clinton, I wondered whether he knew that some of those same people felt personally insulted by the way he'd talked about them.

Nor did Obama's presidency address black people's circumstances as it might have. Dramatic racial wealth disparities, perhaps the most important contributor to black stagnation, persisted largely unchanged. White families in the lowest income quintile have slightly more wealth than black families in the middle quintiles of the income distribution. Intergenerational wealth transfers are among the most significant determinants of familial wealth, and government policies have systematically denied many black families the opportunity to build intergenerational wealth for nearly all of this country's existence. President Obama did not specifically address that history from the podium or through his policy.

Those Americans who lived through state-sponsored terrorism during the Civil Rights Movement wept openly at President Obama's election. But his presidency did not realize the fullest promise of the Civil Rights Movement, which is to say that he did not speak the naked truth about America's devastation of its black communities, a truth that Civil Rights Movement leaders relentlessly pressed upon the nation's conscience. Of course, he never could have been that president. Such a president could only have been elected by an American people willing to entrust the authority of the federal government to someone intent on leveraging its power to repair the damages it has wrought upon black families for generations. Americans elected President Obama out of a genuine desire to prove themselves beyond the evils of racism, and then used his election as proof of our arrival at a mythical "post-racial" utopia while steadfastly denying any evidence to the contrary.

And yet, though my efforts to grapple with the value of feeling represented by this black president force me to acknowledge difficult realities, they inevitably lead me back to one basic truth: I know that I am proud of him. I am proud because I know that he's weathered some of the vitriol he's suffered for no reason other than that he is black. I often wonder if my country yet loves its black people, and by extension, whether it loves me. Sometimes I fear that the answer is no. This is at once terribly frightening and utterly exhausting. I know I am not alone in this. To think that President

Obama has served this country with every ounce of his vigor while perhaps carrying that same fear is to know that he is endowed with fortitude far beyond my own.

I am also thankful for him, because he chose to associate with black people. History will always show that the first black president was a president who embraced black people. This was not a given and should not be taken for granted. His was the first White House that black Americans could visit and feel that they truly belonged. Barack Obama was the first president with whom I felt kinship, not because our skin was similarly colored but because we shared a culture. The President of the United States argued the merits of Drake and Kendrick Lamar the way I do, played pickup basketball with his friends the way I do, and professed his love to his partner with Al Green songs the way I do. Perhaps the simplest way to explain what it means to feel represented by him is to say that I saw myself in him.

The racist fiction of black inferiority has survived the existence of scores of exemplary black people, and it is not only non-black people who have proven susceptible to that toxic propaganda. It is near impossible to go through life hearing that people like you are less intelligent, less capable, and less deserving without that logic seeping into your consciousness. But for every day of my adult life, the leader of the free world has been a black man. It is not enough, then, to say that I saw myself in President Obama. Perhaps more importantly, I saw President Obama in me. This has been the truest value of representation throughout his presidency: not to change the racist's mind about me, but to change my mind about myself.

Representation alone cannot end black people's suffering, but its power cannot be dismissed. I felt that power when I called out to President Obama from the crowd and he responded directly to me. I felt it again when he came down from the stage to greet the audience and shook my outstretched hand.

Most of all, I felt it in the moments just after he disappeared into the night. As I turned away from the stage, I saw the young man with the curly hair and bouncing shoulders. We hadn't yet spoken to each other, but in that moment we knew each other as brothers born of shared experience. And so we hugged, in the way that black men often do: right hands clasped together and held tightly to our chests, left arms wrapped around each other's shoulders, left hands balled into fists and pressed into each other's backs. We hugged, two young men with kinky hair and skin that is so brown as to be considered black.

I said aloud, "We just saw the most powerful man in the world. And he was black."

He replied, "I know. It's crazy. We here."

Mixedness

by E. Dolores Johnson

What a privilege it must be for people to be able to identify you, to place you correctly in the American mosaic with just one look. Not to have them stare quizzically at your face, or ask , "What are you?" like they have a right to know. How comfortable it must be to live without being on guard for the stream of strangers who mistake your identity for some other group and disturb your sense of self.

But I wouldn't know. Because my mixed black-white looks, olive skin, and curly hair confuse people. So much so that their questions and assumptions about me have become a tiresome intrusion to be borne.

Sometimes the misidentification is maddening. Like the time a white gas station attendant where I filled up regularly stuck his head and stale smoker's breath too close to my open window to ask, "You Spanish?"

When I said no, he kept on down the list. "Eye-Talian?" No. "Injun?" No. "You ain't a Jew, are you?" No. "Then what? Tell me," he said.

"Black," I said.

He ordered me to get out of the car so he could take a good look, reaching for the door handle.

"You better step the hell out of my way if you don't want your foot run over," I snapped, then peeled out of the station.

Nearly forty years later, I experienced a slightly more polite repetition of this line of questioning 1,500 miles away. The confused party was a perplexed East Indian gas attendant. When I said I was black, his "Oh!" sounded like that of a student learning the right answer to a pop quiz. Irritating as it was to be the object of curiosity, I wondered how an obvious immigrant — brown, wearing a turban and speaking heavily accented English, didn't understand my distaste at such a challenge.

Sometimes being misidentified goes beyond simply being irritating to have larger ramifications on my life. At an annual physical, I was handed a printout of the day's vitals and information about further appointments. I glanced over the fine print and noticed racial categories listed. Mine was marked white. Was the mark a careless mistake that failed to capture our prior conversation about treating sun spots due to the extra melanin in my mixed race skin? Or had he simply made an assumption when I'd first walked into the room? What if I'd had symptoms of sickle cell anemia or lupus, diseases more common in African Americans? Would he have missed that possibility because he thought I was white?

Then again, my misidentification might be to my advantage. Last spring, when the sun shone brightly, I drove absentmindedly on a straightaway until an intimidating motorcycle policeman in sunglasses pulled me over and said I was speeding. I fidgeted behind the wheel, thinking about points added to my license and increased insurance rates while watching him pull out a form and write me up. But he handed me a warning, not a ticket. But there it was again. When I read over the form, he'd checked my race as white. Couldn't he see I sported an afro to make a statement?

But what if he *had* seen me as black? Would he have penalized me, profiled me, handed me a ticket instead of a warning? Statistics on the harsher penalties police impose on blacks made me wonder, shamefacedly, if being taken for white is a privilege. And to the extent I do get those extra passes, although I've never asked for them, darker African Americans have resented me. Should I accept those misperceptions or keep protesting that no, I'm black? And if I accept those misperceptions, or just let them go to end the whole uncomfortable business, am I selling out, as I know some black people would think?

If I am going to confess, there are times when my misidentification brings out the worst in me. One night, in a cab in midtown Manhattan, I suddenly spotted my destination, blocks ahead of where I'd told the cabbie it was. He stopped on the wide avenue where he could — on the opposite side of the street. I pushed open the cab door on the traffic side without looking. Whoosh! A brown Hispanic man on a bike swerved narrowly around my door.

"Dumb white bitch!" he yelled at me, pedaling away into the night.

So frustrated to be insulted by another person of color, I stood in the street shouting after him. "I'm not white! I'm NOT white."

When I recounted this episode later to a friend, he asked me, "He called you a 'dumb white bitch.' But, of those three insulting names, the only one that offended you was being called *white*?"

It was. Street talking people used 'dumb' and 'bitch' so commonly as put downs for minor disagreements I was able to dismiss both with minor irritation. But, knowing first-hand the vitriol people of color use against white people, I couldn't bear to be seen as white. Or to hear a brown person lob his version of "what are you" at me. And just as painful, standing on that rainy Manhattan street, I was made to feel the white half of me, the white side that America buried with the one drop rule and the irrelevance assigned my white mother's race. I'd always known that my black father made me a black person. So what other reaction could I have had to being called white when black was all that had ever mattered?

What I wish is that people would identify me as a person, and accept my mixedness as unremarkable. That gas attendants, police, and aggrieved bikers would let me be both races and not need to categorize me. That those who need to know my specific racial background, like doctors, would inquire, note and act on its pertinence.

As America's mixed race population grows, as the Census predicts it will, I look forward to when people won't stare at me, misidentify me, or ask "what are you."

How grand that will feel. I can't wait.

Inauguration Day, 2017

by Kim Stafford

The new patriot is a listener.
The new citizen talks to strangers.
The new continental congress convenes
at bus stops, taverns and cafes, parking lots
where neighbors pause (their shopping carts
with flour, milk, and eggs), to speak of justice,
honor, and honesty — while far to the east
a speech is being given in a foreign tongue.

Stand and Bow Down

by Kim Stafford

"Keep your voice down and your head up
when trouble comes," my father said.
"Shouting leads to blows, and blows
to everyone losing what the fight was for."

I see the sturdy tree stand tall, then bend
when wind comes. I watch grass outlast the storm.
When a leader shouts, you have to listen better
than he knows how. You have to be what he might

learn to say, if you are eloquent in witness.

Note: Kim Stafford's father, poet William Stafford, was interned
as a pacifist in World War II and nearly hung for his beliefs by an
mob in Arkansas in 1943. He spent the balance of his life writing
and witnessing for peace, producing a body of poems, teachings,
and questions that faced the propaganda and coercion of the
McCarthy era and the Cold War. "Tyrants depend on followers,"
he wrote, exhorting us to stand up and speak out when the values
of fact, justice, and humane treatment of fellow human beings is at
stake.

When Things Go Wrong, Do Right: Options for Action
by Kim Stafford

Thoughts in response to a friend asking, after grand catastrophe: "What can we do?"

We ask each other in times of trouble: "What can we do — about the Election ... about Global Warming ... about Terrorism ... about ISIS ... about Hitler ... about Genghis Khan...?" Here are some possible responses that occur to me, in a kind of ascending order of usefulness — though it's hard to say what a best response might be, as each is fraught with complexity:

1. You can declare war — on a person, or a nation. You can abdicate true leadership, abandon diplomacy, saying in your haste, "All alternatives to violence have been exhausted." You can let yourself get mad and go kill people.

Occasional national response ... often lamented later.

2. You can turn away — ignore or deny the problem.

Frequent majority response.

3. You can let your emotions be so overwhelming that you become part of the problem — fury, sorrow, despair. Then other people have to add saving you to their existing concerns, instead of working on the problem together.

> *If we can avoid this, it's a good start. Thus, taking care of yourself in the face of difficult news is a high priority, and ultimately a generous act.*

4. You can suffer in silence — which makes you less effective in all ways, for terrorism or demagoguery has worked: You are terrified.

> *Frequent individual response.*

5. You can send money — to a friend, or to someone involved at a personal level, or to an agency positioned to address the problem.

> *This can offer practical help, but also may "buy off" your responsibility to do something more effective.*

6. You can think — Meditate on the situation, address it in your mind, seeking some form of clarity. This can help you identify truly useful action. Or you can think with others: Talk with friends, and then with people you encounter or seek out. Listen carefully. Ponder deeply together. Foster the ripple effect of thought.

> *Individual option* — *then the beginning of action beyond yourself.*

7. You can write about it — make art, respond creatively in order to settle your own emotions and explore solutions through lively imagination, not brute reaction. You can send forth your writing or art to help others see a new angle: a poem, an essay, a letter to the editor, an open letter to both sides.

This can be a useful companion to other forms of response. If you speak your mind, you are likely to get some cruel, even threatening reactions, as the world is a crazy place. But you will also empower others, and gather companions for the difficult, restorative work to come.

8. You can bear witness — through your writing, or in person. Stand in the street with a sign. Stand before the house of the decider. Directly address someone "on the other side."

The beginning of individual active engagement with the problem. Much of the work here is finding a place, a vantage point that can give your individual voice some leverage — not just a voice crying in the wilderness.

9. You can demonstrate with others — You can join a peace walk. You can join a vigil at a prison, at a legislative session, at the gates to The Citadel. Together, you can stand in the path of the White Train.

Physical activism by individuals in groups — undertaking some danger to make a point, and to make news.

10. You can go to the place of trouble — and dwell there, trying to do something about it. You can be the personal ambassador, the seeker, the traveler with a mission — be St. Francis walking to Rome to engage the Pope, or St. Francis undertaking his solo peace "crusade" to meet directly with the Sultan. This approach can be an aspect of all travel: the traveler as seeker and witness.

But consider you are "out of your element," likely to miss cultural cues for effective action. You may become a martyr, may become a cause for revenge, making things worse.

11. You can dedicate your life — to fixing this one problem, surrendering all else in obsessive focus on this.

But you will need to ask, Am I truly helping? Am I effective for change, or only trying to feel better about myself?

12. Instead of reacting against a distant problem, you can seek the causes of human cruelty: poverty, ignorance, injustice, our long war against the Earth. Then enter a calling that engages those causes. Work with like-minded people to gentle the climate of human affairs — by taking on Margaret Mead's old challenge: *Never doubt that a small group of thoughtful, committed citizens can change the world; indeed, it's the only thing that ever has.*

At every point, with every action, practice beauty, imagination, honesty, humor & generosity. Make *what* you seek be *how* you seek.

Reduce despair, and sustain the seeker.

Horizon

by Richard Hoffman

A giant copper moon flares on the lake
in the early dark, and on the car radio, talk.
Talk trying to chew despair. Talk about fear
to hide fear. Talk about talk about talk.
Fifty cents, a dollar a word. It is all just talk

until it isn't. A day may come soon when
we'll have to pay with our lives for the lives
of our friends. What else did we ever have
to pay with? What else were we ever for?
Each ripple on the lake is a lick of flame.

Acknowledgements

"Eyewitness" by Seno Gumira Ajidarma, translated by Jan Lingard. First published in a collection of stories by the same name by ETT Imprint (Australia) in 1995. This permutation of the translation was published by the Lontar Foundation of Jakarta in 2015, also in a collection titled *Eyewitness*. Reprinted with permission from the Lontar Foundation.

"You Had Me at Beheading: The Author of *Against Football* Responds to Selected Hate Mail" Copyright @ 2015 by Steve Almond. First published in The Rumpus, December 1, 2015. Reprinted with permission from the author.

The Lost Family Copyright © 2018 by Jenna Blum. Excerpt reprinted with permission from Harper, an imprint of HarperCollins Publishers.

"Pornograph with Americana" Copyright @ 2016 by Jaswinder Bolina. First published in Omniverse, December, 2016. Reprinted with permission from the author.

"Supremacy" Copyright @ 2017 by Jaswinder Bolina. First published in The Miami Rail, April 2017. Reprinted with permission from the author.

"Rubble City, Rubble Clinic" Copyright @ 2017 by Jaswinder Bolina. First published in Pinwheel, Summer 2017. Reprinted with permission from the author.

"Natalie Said" Copyright @ 2018 by Kelle Groom. First published in What Rough Beast, March 6, 2018. Reprinted with permission from the author.

"River of Grass" Copyright @ 2018 by Kelle Groom. First published in The Cincinnati Review, May 23, 2018. Reprinted with permission from the author.

"An excerpt from 'Defenses'" Copyright @ 2017 by Krysten Hill. First published in *apt*, 2017. Reprinted with permission from the author.

"Are You a Self-Identified Black Woman" Copyright @ 2016 by Krysten

Contributors

Seno Gumira Ajidarma is a writer and journalist who lectures in the Jakarta Institute of the Arts (IKJ) and the Faculty of Humanities, University of Indonesia (UI). He writes political columns regularly in Koran Tempo and panajournal.com. His fiction and non-fiction have won awards including the SEA Write Award, Dinny O'Hearn Prize for literary translation and the Khatulistiwa Award. In 2013, he received a Cultural Award from Indonesia's Ministry of Education and Culture. "Eyewitness" is the title story from *Saksi Mata* or *Eyewitness*, a collection that powerfully dramatizes abuse of power under an autocratic regime.

Kazim Ali was born in the United Kingdom to Muslim parents of Indian, Iranian and Egyptian descent. He received a B.A. and M.A. from the University of Albany-SUNY, and an M.F.A. from New York University. His books encompass several volumes of poetry, including *Sky Ward,* winner of the Ohioana Book Award in Poetry; *The Far Mosque,* winner of Alice James Books' New England/New York Award; *The Fortieth Day; All One's Blue;* and the cross-genre text *Bright Felon.* His novels include the recently published *The Secret Room: A String Quartet* and among his books of essays is *Fasting for Ramadan: Notes from a Spiritual Practice.* Ali is an associate professor of Creative Writing and Comparative Literature at Oberlin College. His new book of poems, *Inquisition,* and a new hybrid memoir, *Silver Road: Essays, Maps & Calligraphies,* were both released in 2018.

Steve Almond does a lot of stuff. He's the author of nine books of fiction and nonfiction, including the New York Times bestsellers *Candyfreak* and *Against Football.* His new book, *Bad Stories,* is a literary investigation of what the hell just happened to our country. He wrote it to keep from going crazy. He hosts the New York Times "Dear Sugars" podcast with his pal Cheryl Strayed. His short stories have been anthologized widely, in the *Best American Short Stories, The Pushcart Prize, Best American Erotica,* and *Best American Mysteries* series. He also publishes crazy, DIY books. He'll come to your town if you ask.

Elorm Avakame is a resident physician at Children's National Medical Center in Washington, DC. He was previously a MD/Master's in Public Policy student at Harvard Medical School and the Harvard Kennedy School, where he was a Sheila C. Johnson Leadership Fellow at the HKS

Center for Public Leadership.

Jenna Blum (@Jenna_Blum) is the New York Times and internationally bestselling author of *Those Who Save Us* and *The Lost Family*, one novel examining the rise of fascism and the other its consequences. She is one of Oprah's Top 30 Women Writers and a proud member of the Resistance. For more, please visit www.jennablum.com.

Jaswinder Bolina's latest collection of poems *The 44th of July* is forthcoming from Omnidawn in spring 2019. He is author of two previous books, *Phantom Camera* (2013) and *Carrier Wave* (2007), and of the digital chapbook *The Tallest Building in America* (2014). He teaches on the faculty of the MFA Program in Creative Writing at the University of Miami.

Sari Boren is a writer and museum exhibit developer who has worked on over 50 museum exhibits across the country. Her essays have been published in Copper Nickel, Lilith Magazine, The Southeast Review, Alimentum, and Hobart, among others, and she's a member of the Totally New Theater Playwrights' Collective at the Marblehead Little Theater. Sari teaches creative nonfiction at Grub Street and is a co-manager of the Four Stories reading series.

Stephanie Burt is Professor of English at Harvard and author of three poetry collections, *Belmont, Parallel Play*, and *Popular Music*, and several collections of critical works. Her essay collection *Close Calls with Nonsense* was a finalist for the National Book Critics Circle Award. Her other works include *Advice from the Lights; The Poem is You: 60 Contemporary American Poems and How to Read Them; The Art of the Sonnet; Something Understood: Essays and Poetry for Helen Vendler; The Forms of Youth: Adolescence and 20th Century Poetry; Randall Jarrell on W. H. Auden;* and *Randall Jarrell and His Age*. Her writing has appeared in the New York Times Book Review, the London Review of Books, the Times Literary Supplement, The Believer, and the Boston Review.

Anne Champion is the author of *The Good Girl is Always a Ghost* (Black Lawrence Press, 2018), *Reluctant Mistress* (Gold Wake Press, 2013), and *The Dark Length Home* (Noctuary Press, 2017). Her poems have appeared in Verse Daily, Prairie Schooner, Salamander, Crab Orchard Review, Epiphany Magazine, The Pinch, The Greensboro Review, New South, and elsewhere. She was an 2009 Academy of American Poet's Prize recipient, a Barbara Deming Memorial grant recipient, a 2015 Best of the Net winner, and a Pushcart Prize nominee. She teaches writing and literature at Wheelock College in Boston, MA.

Kendra DeColo is the author of *My Dinner with Ron Jeremy* (Third Man Books, 2016) and *Thieves in the Afterlife* (Saturnalia Books, 2014), selected by Yusef Komunyakaa for the 2013 Saturnalia Books Poetry Prize. Her poems and essays appear in Tin House, Waxwing, Los Angeles Review, Gulf Coast, Bitch Magazine, VIDA, and elsewhere. She is co-host of the podcast RE/VERB: A Third Man Books Production and she lives in Nashville, Tennessee.

Jeanne Dietsch was a columnist for Robotics & Automation magazine from 2009-2012, while she was CEO of MobileRobots Inc. After selling that company, she earned an MPA at The Harvard Kennedy School. She just won the Democratic primary for State Senate against two contenders, and expects to be elected to the New Hampshire Senate in November.

Boyah J. Farah is a refugee turned writer from Somalia whose works of nonfiction have been featured in The Guardian, Salon, WGBH, Harvard Transition, Grub Daily, Somerville Times, and Truthdig. A Judy Layzer Fellow, he participated in the Memoir Incubator at GrubStreet Creative Writing School in Boston.

Robbie Gamble holds an MFA in poetry from Lesley University. His poems are out or forthcoming in Scoundrel Time, MassPoetry, Writers Resist, Solstice, Poet Lore, and RHINO. He was the winner of the 2017 Carve Poetry prize. He lives in Brookline, Massachusetts, and works as a nurse practitioner caring for homeless people in Boston.

Kat Geddes is a global health activist and lawyer whose secret loves are spoken word poetry and Union Square donuts. When she's not in sub-Saharan Africa promoting access to medicines, you can find her hunched over a black coffee in Tatte, scribbling poems, or sketching cartoons about racism, feminism, and woke squirrels. She has performed at the Lizard Lounge, won poetry slams at the Nuyorican Poets Cafe in New York, and formed her own spoken word group, the Live Poets Society. Her poems and sketches can be found @karrotsandpeas.

Regie Gibson is a poet, songwriter, author, workshop facilitator, and educator who has performed, taught, and lectured at schools, universities, theaters and various other venues on two continents and in seven countries. Most recently in Havana, Cuba. Regie and his work appear in the New Line Cinema film love jones, based largely on events in his life. The poem entitled "Brother to the Night (A Blues for Nina)" appears on the movie soundtrack and is performed by the film's star, Larenz Tate. Regie performed "Hey Nappyhead" in the film with world-renowned percussionist and composer Kahil El Zabar, composer of the score for the musical The Lion King.

Kelle Groom is the author of four poetry collections: *Spill, Five Kingdoms, Luckily* (Anhinga Press), and *Underwater City* (University Press of Florida). Her work has appeared in AGNI, American Poetry Review, Best American Poetry, The New Yorker, The New York Times, Ploughshares, and Poetry, among other journals. Groom's memoir, *I Wore the Ocean in the Shape of a Girl* (Simon & Schuster), is a Barnes & Noble Discover selection, a New York Times Book Review Editor's Choice selection, a Library Journal Best Memoir, an Oprah O Magazine selection, and an Oxford American Editor's Pick. An NEA Literature Fellow, Groom is on the faculty of the low-residency MFA Program at Sierra Nevada College, Lake Tahoe, and director of the Summer Workshops at the Fine Arts Work Center in Provincetown.

Krysten Hill received her MFA in poetry from UMass Boston where she currently teaches. Her work can be found in apt, The Baltimore Review, B O D Y, Boiler Magazine, Up the Staircase Quarterly, Word Riot, Muzzle, PANK, Tinderbox Poetry Journal, Winter Tangerine Review and elsewhere. She is the recipient of the 2016 St. Botolph Club Foundation Emerging Artist Award. Her chapbook, *How Her Spirit Got Out*, received the 2017 Jean Pedrick Chapbook Prize. For more, please visit www.krystenhill.com.

Brenda Hillman has been an active part of the Bay Area literary community since 1975. She has published several chapbooks and is the author of ten full-length collections from Wesleyan University Press, the most recent of which are *Practical Water* (2009), winner of the Los Angeles Times Book Award, *Seasonal Works with Letters on Fire* (2013), which received the International Griffin Poetry Prize for 2014 and the Northern California Book Award, and *Extra Hidden Life, among the Days* (2018). Hillman has also received the William Carlos Williams Prize from Poetry Society of America and the Academy of American Poets Fellowship. With Patricia Dienstfrey, she co-edited *The Grand Permission: New Writings on Poetics and Motherhood* (Wesleyan, 2003). Hillman, a mother and a grandmother, is married to poet Robert Hass. She is the Olivia C. Filippi Professor of Poetry at St. Mary's College in Moraga California. For several decades, Hillman has worked as an activist for social and environmental justice.

Richard Hoffman is the author of seven books, including the celebrated *Half the House: a Memoir*, published in a 20th Anniversary Edition in 2015, and the 2014 memoir *Love & Fury*. In addition to the volume *Interference and Other Stories*, he has published four collections of poetry: *Without Paradise; Gold Star Road; Emblem;* and *Noon until Night*. He is Senior Writer in Residence at Emerson College and an Adjunct Associate Professor at Columbia University.

Jennifer Jean's debut poetry collection is *The Fool* (Big Table). Her new manuscript, titled *OBJECT*, was a finalist for the 2016 Green Mountains Review Book Prize. She is the recipient of Waxwing Journal's first annual Good Bones Prize, and she received an Ambassador for Peace Award in 2013 for her activism in the arts. Jennifer's work has appeared in: Poetry, Crab Creek Review, Rattle, Denver Quarterly, Green Mountains Review, Solstice Magazine, and more. She's Poetry Editor of The Mom Egg Review, Managing Editor of Talking Writing Magazine, and Co-director of Morning Garden Artists Retreats. Jennifer teaches Free2Write poetry workshops to trauma survivors and to sex-trafficking survivors. For more information, visit www.fishwifetales.com.

E. Dolores Johnson's writing on race has appeared or is forthcoming in the Buffalo News, the Writers of Color Anthology, Narratively and Lunch Ticket. Her multi-generational memoir in progress about mixed race life is the story of the browning of America and changing attitudes about race-mixing. She is looking for a publisher. Johnson completed the Memoir Incubator program at Grub Street and studied creative writing at Harvard's Nieman Foundation. She has been awarded residencies at Djerassi, Blue Mountain Center, Ragdale, and the VCCA and is available to do readings. She has consulted on diversity for think tanks, universities, corporations and nonprofits. Johnson holds an MBA from Harvard University and a BA from Howard University. Her work can be read at e.doloresjohnson.com. Follow her on twitter@ elladolo and FB.

Sebastian Johnson is a philanthropic strategist and policy advocate whose writing has been featured in The Washington Post and The Los Angeles Times, among other publications. In 2016, Sebastian delivered a TEDxMidAtlantic talk titled "The Case for the Basic Income." Sebastian is a graduate of the Harvard Kennedy School of Government and Georgetown University. His areas of interest include criminal justice reform, taxation and economic policy, and access to educational opportunity.

Sonya Larson's short fiction and essays have appeared in *Best American Short Stories 2017*, American Short Fiction, American Literary Review, Poets & Writers, Writer's Chronicle, Audible.com, West Branch, Salamander, Memorious, Solstice Magazine, Del Sol Review, Red Mountain Review, The Hub, and more. She has received honors and fellowships from the Bread Loaf Writers' Conference, Vermont Studio Center, University of Wisconsin-Madison, St. Botolph Club Foundation, and more. She currently works as Director of the Muse and the Marketplace literary conference, hosted by GrubStreet in Boston, as well as a manager of the Boston Writers of Color Group. She received her MFA in fiction in the Program for Writers at Warren Wilson College. Sonya lives in Somerville, MA, and is currently writing a novel.

Alexandria Marzano-Lesnevich is the author of *The Fact Of A Body: A Murder and a Memoir*, recipient of the 2018 Lambda Literary Award for Lesbian Memoir and the 2018 Chautauqua Prize. Named one of the best books of the year by Entertainment Weekly, Audible.com, Bustle, Book Riot, The Times of London, and The Guardian, it was an Indie Next Pick and a Junior Library Guild selection, long-listed for the Gordon Burn Prize, shortlisted for the CWA Gold Dagger, and a finalist for a New England Book Award and a Goodreads Choice Award. It has been published in the US, the UK, and the Netherlands; translations are forthcoming in Turkey, Korea, Taiwan, Spain, Greece, Brazil, and France. The recipient of fellowships from The National Endowment for the Arts, MacDowell, and Yaddo, as well as a Rona Jaffe Award, Marzano-Lesnevich lives in Portland, Maine and is an Assistant Professor of English at Bowdoin College.

Jan Lingard before retirement, had a long career teaching Indonesian at the Australian National University and at The University of Sydney. Her literary translations include *The Outlaw and Other Stories* and *Diverse Lives* (both published by Oxford University Press) and *Eyewitness* (Imprint), winner of the Victorian Premier's Prize for Literary Translation, 1997. She is the author of *Refugees and Rebels*. (Australian Scholarly Publishing, 2008)

Fred Marchant is the author of five books of poetry, the most recent of which is *Said Not Said* (2017). Earlier books include *The Looking House, Full Moon Boat*, and *House on Water, House in Air*. His first book, *Tipping Point*, won the 1993 Washington Prize, and was reissued in a 20th anniversary second edition. Marchant has co-translated works by Vietnamese poets

Tran Dang Khoa and Vo Que. He has also edited *Another World Instead: The Early Poems of William Stafford*. An emeritus professor of English, he is the founding director of the Suffolk University Poetry Center in Boston. He is the winner of the May Sarton Award from the New England Poetry Club, given to poets "whose work is an inspiration to other writers."

Timothy Patrick McCarthy (@DrTPM) is an award-winning scholar, writer, educator, and activist who has taught on the faculty at Harvard University since 2005. Twice named one of Harvard Crimson's "Professors of the Year," Dr. McCarthy is also the Stanley Paterson Professor of American History in the Boston Clemente Course, a college humanities program for low-income adults in Dorchester, MA, and co-recipient of the 2015 National Humanities Medal. He is the author or editor of five books from the New Press, including *Stonewall's Children: Living Queer History in the Age of Liberation, Loss, and Love*, forthcoming in Spring 2019. A board member of the American Repertory Theater, he is the host of *Resistance Mic!* and director of the A.R.T. of Human Rights series. For more, please visit https://www.hks.harvard.edu/faculty/timothy-patrick-mccarthy.

Lena Merhej, PhD, is a visual storyteller and an expert in graphic narration. She taught at several universities in Beirut, directed Beirut Animated, worked with Tosh Fesh to promote comics and founded the Story Center. She is also a co-founder and a member of Samandal, an award winning comics organization in Lebanon. Lena illustrated over 25 Arabic children's books and has exhibited her work internationally. Some of her award winning projects are the animation *Drawing the War* (2002), the comic book, *Kamen Sine (Another Year)* (2009), the graphic novel *Mrabba w Labban (Yogurt and Jam or how my mother became Lebanese)* (2011), and the picture book *Boustani ain anta (My Orchard, where are you?)*. Recent comics she worked on are *Là où il y a la vie, il y a l'amour (Where there is life, there is love)* (2017) for Solidarités International and *Manarat* (2017) for OXFAM. She is now working on a book about being an Arab in Marseille.

Vi Khi Nao is the author of *Sheep Machine* (Black Sun Lit, 2018) and *Umbilical Hospital* (Press 1913, 2017) and *The Old Philosopher*, which won the Nightboat Books Prize for Poetry in 2014. Her short story collection, *A Brief Alphabet of Torture*, won FC2's Ronald Sukenick Innovative Fiction Prize in 2016. Her debut novel is *Fish in Exile* (Coffee House Press, 2016). Vi Khi Nao's work includes poetry, fiction, film and cross-genre collaboration. Her stories, poems, and drawings have appeared in NOON, Ploughshares , Black Warrior Review and BOMB, among others. She holds an MFA in fiction from Brown University.

Robert Pinsky is a poet, essayist, translator, teacher, and speaker. He is the author of nineteen books, most of which are collections of his poetry. His first two terms as United States Poet Laureate were marked by such visible dynamism—and such national enthusiasm in response—that the Library of Congress appointed him to an unprecedented third term. Throughout his career, Pinsky has been dedicated to identifying and invigorating poetry's place in the world. Known worldwide, Pinsky's work has earned him the PEN/Voelcker Award, the William Carlos Williams Prize, the Lenore Marshall Prize, Italy's Premio Capri, the Korean Manhae Award, and the Harold Washington Award from the City of Chicago, among other accolades.

Bruce Robinson's recent work appears or is forthcoming in Mobius, Fourth River/Tributaries, Cleaver (Life as Activism), Blueline, Journal of Compressed Creative Arts, the Indolent Books What Rough Beast series, dispatchespoetrywars, Panoply, and South Florida Poetry Journal. He appreciates the good offices of Atlantic Center for the Arts, the Key West Literary Workshops, and the Brooklyn and Albany, NY public libraries.

Shanoor Seervai works as a researcher and writer at the Commonwealth Fund, a national philanthropy dedicated to supporting affordable and accessible health care for all. She received a Master in Public Policy degree from the Harvard Kennedy School of Government (HKS) in 2017, where her research focused on child and youth protection in the ongoing refugee crisis. At HKS, Shanoor was a Freedman/Martin journalism scholar and served as the Editor-in-Chief of the Kennedy School Review. Before coming to HKS, she reported for The Wall Street Journal in India.

Kim Stafford is the founding director of the Northwest Writing Institute at Lewis & Clark College, and author of a dozen books of poetry and prose, including *Having Everything Right: Essays of Place, 100 Tricks Every Boy Can Do: How My Brother Disappeared*, and *The Muses Among Us: Eloquent Listening and Other Pleasures of the Writer's Craft*. For more about Kim Stafford's music, writing, and films go to www.kim-stafford.com.

Grace Talusan is the winner of the 2017 Restless Books Prize for New Immigrant Writing for Nonfiction for her memoir *The Body Papers*, set for publication in spring 2019. She was born in the Philippines and raised in New England. Talusan graduated from Tufts University and the MFA Program in Writing at UC Irvine. She is the recipient of a U.S. Fulbright Fellowship to the Philippines and an Artist Fellowship Award from the Massachusetts Cultural Council. Talusan teaches at Grub Street and Tufts.

Nick Thorkelson is a cartoonist living in Boston. "Marcuse on the MTA" is an excerpt from *Herbert Marcuse, Philosopher of Utopia: A Graphic Biography*, forthcoming from City Lights Books in spring 2019. He has done cartoons on local politics for The Boston Globe and in support of organizations working on economic justice, peace, and public health. He is the co-author and/or illustrator of *The Earth Belongs to the People, The Underhanded History of the USA, The Legal Rights of Union Stewards, The Comic Strip of Neoliberalism,* and *Economic Meltdown Funnies,* and has contributed to a number of nonfiction comics anthologies. He is working on a graphic novel about the end of the Sixties, *A Better World Is Possible.* Nick also moonlights as a musician, animator, graphic designer, and painter.

Maisie Wiltshire-Gordon is fascinated by how language works and the ways we put it to use. She is looking for answers through storytelling, philosophy, and everyday conversation. As a strategy consultant, she is particularly interested in the role narrative has to play in business transformation. Maisie lives in Cambridge, MA.

ABOUT PANGYRUS

Pangyrus is a Boston-based group of writers, editors, and artists with a new vision for how high-quality creative work can prosper online and in print. We aim to foster a community of individuals and organizations dedicated to art, ideas, and making culture thrive.

Combining Pangaea and gyrus, the terms for the world continent and whorls of the cerebral cortex crucial to verbal association, Pangyrus is about connection.

INDEX by AUTHOR and GENRE

ESSAYS

FICTION AND COMICS

CPSIA information can be obtained
at www.ICGtesting.com
Printed in the USA
FFHW020612271118
49660965-54034FF